JESUS ON

M🜲NEY

Book 3 – Crossing the Finish Line

LARRY BURKETT
WITH KAY MOORE

PRODUCTION TEAM

Gene Mims, *President, LifeWay Church Resources*
Michael D. Miller, *Director, Church Leadership Group*
Gary L. Aylor, *Director, Church Stewardship Services*
J. David Carter, *Lead Stewardship Specialist*
Norma J. Goldman, *Editorial Team Leader*
Linda W. Grammer, *Assistant Editor*

We gratefully acknowledge the contributions of Michael E. Taylor
to the development of this manuscript.

ISBN 0-6330-0304-2

Dewey Decimal Classification: 248.6
Subject Heading: JESUS CHRIST—TEACHINGS\STEWARDSHIP\DEVOTIONAL LITERATURE

Printed in the United States of America

Unless otherwise indicated, all Scripture quotations are from
The Holy Bible, *New International Version*,
Copyright © 1973, 1978, 1984 by International Bible Society

Other Scripture quotations are from
The NEW AMERICAN STANDARD BIBLE
© Copyright The Lockman Foundation,
1960, 1962, 1963, 1968, 1971, 1972, 1973, 1975, 1977, 1995
Used by Permission.

Church Stewardship Services
LifeWay Church Resources
127 Ninth Avenue, North
Nashville, TN 37234

TABLE OF CONTENTS

Crossing the finish line! It's a concept most of us can easily identify with because athletics are so much a part of our culture. We can picture a strong, lean youth pressing hard toward the finish line just ahead. We cheer wildly from the sidelines, urging the athlete on to victory! What an exciting image for a child of God! Paul drew just such a picture of the day when our own race has ended and we will appear before God to receive the victor's crown!

We pray that your study of *Jesus On Money* thus far has inspired you to run the race like never before. In Book 1, *Charting a New Course*, you discovered God's principles for managing all the resources entrusted to your care. As you established a spending plan and began to practice good financial management habits, you saw new opportunities to partner with God in accomplishing His purposes.

Through Book 2, *Making Mid-Course Corrections*, you learned how to adjust your financial management plans to fit the changing circumstances of life. You discovered the tremendous importance of setting goals to line up with God's specific plan for your life, your family, and your future.

Now you are embarking on a great spiritual adventure as you determine God's unique purpose as He works through your finances, circumstances, and opportunities. Many people never discover the real reason God provides abundance. They cannot see how their lives can actually be part of ushering in the kingdom of God. Through *Jesus On Money: Crossing the Finish Line* you will learn these truths, and more!

God has a plan to reconcile the world to Himself. Amazingly, we can be part of that plan. Through this study, you will gain a clear picture of how you can impact the world for Christ. Accomplishing the goal of the Great Commission is more about obedience and faith than it is about money. Through simple obedience, and the wise use of all the resources entrusted to your care, you are a living testimony of the power of Christ to change a life, a family, and a world!

Gary L. Aylor, Director
Church Stewardship Services

JESUS ON

MONEY

Book 3 – Crossing the Finish Line

INTRODUCTION

"When I was a child, I talked like a child, I thought like a child, I reasoned like a child. When I became a man, I put childish ways behind me."

–1 Corinthians 13:11

In this stewardship series, I trust you have completed Book 1, *Jesus On Money: Charting a New Course*, and Book 2, *Jesus On Money: Making Mid-Course Corrections*. By applying the principles you learned to your personal finances, you have taken significant steps toward growing in faithful stewardship in the eyes of Jesus Christ.

I want to congratulate you for starting Book 3, *Jesus On Money: Crossing the Finish Line*. In 1 Corinthians 13:11, at left, the apostle Paul makes it very clear that mature believers have learned to put away childish things that complicate their lives. How well that admonition applies to money management for Christians! This study may be the most challenging of the three books for you simply because it teaches what the lifestyle of a financially free person looks like. Jesus Christ calls you to nothing less than sacrificially following Him in all arenas of life, including money management.

Financial freedom is not some secret strategy to make you more wealthy or more comfortable with worldly goods. Neither is it God's ultimate aim to cater to your comforts here on earth while the rest of the world suffers and goes to hell by the millions. Rather, the clear goal of financial freedom is to grow in faithfulness to God's purposes here on earth.

"And he died for all, that those who live should no longer live for themselves but for him who died for them and was raised again" (2 Corinthians 5:15). Make no mistake — mature believers will both *hear* the call to sacrificial living from the Master and promptly *obey* Him. Christ's own example is that of pouring Himself out for the world (Philippians 2:7-8). Faithful believers will do no less.

The topics for the next six weeks cause my heart to race a little faster because each represents a key element of mature Christian stewardship:

- Sacrificial Giving
- Living with Abundance
- Uses of Wealth
- Leaving a Legacy
- A Long Look at Retirement
- Fulfilling the Great Commission

I believe the most critical need in God's church today is leadership — men and women who will stand up and lead with integrity — people whose walk matches their talk. America needs, your church needs, people who not only talk about faithful stewardship but who openly model changed and sacrificial living. Younger Christian families can then see what living a sacrificial Christian lifestyle looks like and can learn to follow. Challenge yourself by asking, "Would my church be healthy if all the members adopted my stewardship lifestyle?" Completing *Jesus On Money: Crossing the Finish Line* will equip you with the principles and procedures to model faithful stewardship in your church.

In this book, as with the two previous books, you will employ an interactive learning process. As a refresher, let me remind you that each day, for five days a week, you are asked to study a segment of the material and complete activities that relate to what you just read. Each day's work requires 20 to 30 minutes of study time. Even if you find that you can study the material in less time, spread out the study over five days. This will give you more time to apply the truths to your life.

As with Books 1 and 2, members gather for group sessions at the end of each week's study. The sessions help you reflect on the concepts and experiences in *Jesus On Money* and apply the ideas to your life. You will share insights gained, look for answers to problems encountered, and gain strength from the fact that others are encountering similar struggles and victories.

Although you may benefit from completing the studies totally on your own, without a group experience, you will have missed the critical element Jesus' disciples experienced: relationships with one another in Christ's presence. As members share their own testimonies about growing in stewardship, others give feedback and are encouraged in their own challenges and successes. Therefore, I strongly encourage you to connect with other believers to study this material.

This book has been written as a tutorial text. Study it as if I were sitting at your side, helping you learn. When I ask you a question or give you an assignment, respond immediately. Each assignment appears in **boldface type.** In most cases, I, as your personal tutor, will give you some feedback about your response — for example, a suggestion about what you might have written. This process is designed to help you learn the material more

INTRODUCTION

effectively. Do not deny yourself valuable learning experiences by skipping these activities.

Set a definite time and select a quiet place where you can study with little interruption. Keep a Bible handy for times when the material asks you to look up Scripture. Make notes of problems, questions, or concerns that arise as you study. You will discuss many of these during your group sessions. Write these notes in the margins of this book so you can find them easily.

If you have started a study of *Jesus On Money* and you are not involved in a group study, try to enlist some friends or associates who will work through this course with you. A husband and wife are encouraged to work through the material together. *Jesus On Money Leader Guide* provides guidance and learning activities for these sessions. (Send orders or inquiries to Customer Service Center, 127 Ninth Avenue, North; Nashville, TN 37234; call 1-800-458-2772; or visit your local LifeWay Christian store. Ask for ISBN 0-6330-0308-5.)

As with the Book 1 and Book 2 studies, a key decision continues to be the decision to trust Jesus as your Savior. If you have not done this already, I encourage you to make this decision as the study begins. Within the Week 1 work are helps for making that decision. You will benefit more from this course if you go through the material already having committed your life to Christ. If you're not ready to make that decision just now, be aware that the need for this decision will be an ongoing emphasis. The material gives you opportunity to look at your relationship with Christ and to determine your need to commit your life to Him.

I pray that God will abundantly bless you with strength and wisdom to undertake this study and with the courage and faith to apply what you learn.

Larry Burkett

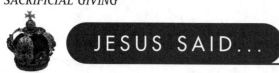

JESUS SAID...

Week 1, Day 1

EXAMINE YOUR COMMITMENT

This Week

Day 1: Examine Your Commitment
Day 2: A Sacrificial Lifestyle
Day 3: A Careful Balance
Day 4: Place God's Kingdom First
Day 5: The Right Attitude

Scripture Verses

"God made him who had no sin to be sin for us, so that in him we might become the righteousness of God."
          –2 Corinthians 5:21

"But when the time had fully come, God sent his Son, born of a woman, born under law, to redeem those under law, that we might receive the full rights of sons."
          –Galatians 4:4-5

Mature Christian living habitually includes sacrifice. I'm not speaking of generous giving or freely sharing from your abundance. By sacrifice I mean choosing to give up something of great value in order to attain something of greater value.

God sacrificed His only Son at the cross. Jesus, of infinite value as a member of the Trinity, died in order to attain an even greater value — the redemption of humankind. See 2 Corinthians 5:21 and Galatians 4:4-5 at left.

In Luke 21:2-4, Jesus praised the widow because she gave so sacrificially — literally, all she had to live on! The rich gave gifts from their abundance, but Jesus particularly called attention to the widow's great sacrifice.

What have you done without lately — not token deprivation but genuine sacrifice, something you would really miss — in order to honor God in your giving? A much needed vacation? The opportunity to purchase a brand-new car or a new, spacious house? When was the last time you gave sacrificially to God rather than out of your abundance? (In Week 2 you'll study about this latter type of giving.)

Does a time immediately come to mind? If so, describe it here.

_____
_____
_____

This week you'll study challenging issues like
- the components of genuine Christian commitment that make sacrifice possible,
- knowing how to make sacrificial adjustment to your lifestyle,
- balancing your family needs with others in even more desperate need, and
- how to keep the proper attitude when you give sacrificially.

What kind of commitment to Christ would prompt you to give until it hurts? A pastor of a large, dynamic church confided that members were critical

Week 1, Day 1

Scripture Verses

because he allowed Sunday services to extend beyond noon when the local professional football team had home games. Sports, recreation, or other activities are not the problem in this church's situation. The problem is a lack of vital, dynamic commitment to God.

Many dedicated Christians are willing to accept God's direction at any moment and surrender their jobs, home, and comforts to accomplish the tasks He assigns them. However, they do not represent a majority within the Christian community. A standard for Christian service that requires little of us yields a sizeable body of believers who never really mature. In God's discipleship plan, some adversity and self-denial are almost certain to be necessary ingredients for spiritual maturity. See James 1:2-4 at right. Luke 14:27 is the very cornerstone of discipleship, and it presumes sacrifice.

"Consider it all joy, my brethren, when you encounter various trials, knowing that the testing of your faith produces endurance. And let endurance have its perfect result, that you may be perfect and complete, lacking in nothing."
—*James 1:2-4, NASB*

A commitment to the lordship of Jesus means that you are willing to go where He determines you can be used best. The Word describes you as a soldier in God's army; see 2 Timothy 2:3-4 at right. It admonishes you to avoid becoming so caught up in the everyday matters of life that you take yourself out of the battle.

Putting God first to the point of sacrifice means the active, daily process of knowing and being known by God. It starts with a thorough understanding of God's handbook for life: the Bible. It requires a heartfelt desire to please God and a willingness to accept God's authority.

"Endure hardship with us, like a good soldier of Christ Jesus. No one serving as a soldier gets involved in civilian affairs — he wants to please his commanding officer."
—*2 Timothy 2:3-4*

Use this as an opportunity to take stock of the time you spend with God. Is a daily quiet time now a regular part of your life? ❑ **Yes** ❑ **No**
If it is, when do you observe it? _____
Where? _____

What is the best experience you have had in your quiet time this week?
_____
_____
_____

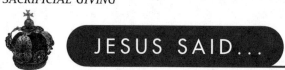

JESUS SAID...

Week 1, Day 1

Scripture Verses

"No servant can serve two masters. Either he will hate the one and love the other, or he will be devoted to the one and despise the other. You cannot serve both God and Money."
–Luke 16:13

"Jesus replied, 'No one who puts his hand to the plow and looks back is fit for service in the kingdom of God.'"
–Luke 9:62

" . . . Whoever sows sparingly will also reap sparingly, and whoever sows generously will also reap generously."
–2 Corinthians 9:6

EXAMINE YOUR COMMITMENT *continued . . .*

Two things last for eternity: the Word of God and human souls. Material goods are simply vehicles for you to use in accomplishing God's work. Jesus said you must make a choice about your commitment, and only two choices exist. See what He says in Luke 16:13 in the margin.

Christ made it pretty clear that He sought those who would commit everything to the service of God's kingdom, to the point of sacrifice. Many people were attracted to Him because of the miracles He performed. Each time they asked Him if they could join His disciples, He directed them to lay aside their own desires and follow Him without reservation. See what Jesus says in Luke 9:62 at left. With few exceptions, they turned back to whatever they had been doing; the price was simply too high for them. How are you sacrificing in the four areas below?

Money — Sometimes you find it is easier to give money than time and talent. I find that a stewardship commitment involves all three. The sowing and reaping principle taught by God's Word in 2 Corinthians 9:6 at left applies to your funds, your abilities, and your time and energies.

Do you give sacrificially? _____

Talents — Many Christians misuse the intellect and abilities God has given by using them exclusively in the pursuit of material success. Others dedicate only a portion of their lives to God's service. But what about giving your talents sacrificially? A speaker I know received an honorarium for conducting a seminar. She had a choice about how to spend it — replacing a well-worn sofa or funding a missions trip for someone who couldn't go otherwise. After prayer, she realized that God intended for her to dedicate the honorarium to kingdom work. See Isaiah 40:8 in far right margin.

List ways that your professional skill can be used in your local church.
_____
_____
_____
_____

Week 1, Day 1

Time — Identify your most precious earthly love. Is it difficult to find time for that person? Do you get to spend enough time with him or her? As with any love relationship, your relationship with Jesus requires time. Evaluate the time you spend on your relationship with Jesus on the scale below. ("0" equals hardly any time at all and "5" represents fantastic quiet time in Bible study and prayer.)

           0   1   2   3   4   5

Are you pleased with the time you're spending? If not, what steps can you take to devote more time to developing your love relationship with Jesus?

_____
_____
_____
_____
_____

Motives — What about your motives for earning a living? Many times a commitment will break down when it requires a sacrifice that may include a career change. A Christian who was an executive with a national hotel chain faced a dilemma. The company he worked for decided to include a pornographic cable system in its rooms. After vocally opposing it, he determined that he must leave the company. At age 60, he knew his decision clearly involved deciding which master he must serve. Today, he is a successful real estate salesperson who seeks to put the Lord first in everything.

See what Jesus says about this type of sacrifice in Luke 12:31 at right. State what you believe Jesus promises in this verse.

_____
_____
_____
_____

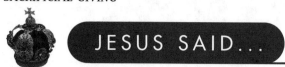

JESUS SAID...

Week 1, Day 1

This Week

EXAMINE YOUR COMMITMENT *continued . . .*

Have you had an experience like that of the hotel executive? If so, tell about it here.

_____

_____

_____

_____

_____

Are you willing to weigh each decision against God's Word and follow the narrow path God requires?

Choose daily to follow Jesus, even when it requires sacrifice. Ask Jesus to make you willing to see that sacrifice is part of His requirement for you as His follower. Your Day-2 study will teach you some specifics of how to do this.

Perhaps as you've studied today's material you realized that you have never really had a personal encounter with Jesus. You know you can't really call yourself His follower, because you have never made a commitment to take that step.

Before you go any further in *Jesus On Money*, it is vitally important that you get this matter settled. Your whole life, including this present study, will take on an entirely different meaning once you have decided to become a follower of Jesus.

Here is how you can do that. Ask yourself if you have ever accepted Jesus as your personal Savior. You must first recognize that everyone who has ever lived is separated from God because of sin. Sin creates a great barrier between a person and God. The Bible tells us, "all have sinned, and come short of the glory of God" (Romans 3:23). It also tells us that the punishment for sin is death (Romans 6:23). The good news is that Jesus voluntarily paid for your sin and mine when He died on the cross! Not only did He die, but also He was raised from the dead. His resurrection proved His power over death and its consequences.

Week 1, Day 1

Notes

When you confess to Him that you have sinned, that you want His forgiveness, and that you understand and accept that He died in payment for your sins, He promises a new life and assures you of a home in heaven when you die!

You might want to pray a simple prayer much like this: *Dear God, I know that Jesus is Your Son and that He died on the cross and was raised from the dead. I know that I am a sinner and need forgiveness. I am willing to turn away from my sins and trust Jesus as my Savior and Lord. Thank You for saving me. In Jesus' name, amen.*

If you prayed that prayer just now, welcome to the family of God! You have just made the most important decision of your life. You can be sure that you are saved and have eternal life. You are beginning a new life as a follower of Christ. Talk to your pastor, a Christian friend, or your *Jesus On Money* group leader about your decision. If you are already a Christian, pause and thank God for new life in Christ. Ask Him to help you exhibit the qualities of a "new creation."

JESUS SAID...

Week 1, Day 2

A SACRIFICIAL LIFESTYLE

S etting worthy goals is easy, but translating them into practice is not so simple. Jesus does call you to sacrifice. But you may be thinking, "How do I incorporate sacrifice into my life? It would be a big leap for me."

A lifestyle of sacrifice may not involve the kind of major leap that you presume. At this point in your *Jesus On Money* study, you may already be further down the road than you think. If you've been putting principles learned into practice, you've already laid the groundwork for stretching yourself even further to become the kind of disciple Jesus wants you to be. You're already working yourself into a pattern of living that characterizes the life of Christ.

For example, you may already be well into the discipline of asking yourself, "How much is enough?" When you start to buy some clothing item, or when you have the urge to eat out again and again, or when you have the option of working overtime to excess, or when you try to decide whether to stay up late watching a movie versus doing your bedtime devotionals, it may already be second nature to say, "Do I really need to do this?"

What are you doing differently now because of your love for Jesus?

_____
_____
_____
_____

If you've been following the financial practices taught in this study, you likely now are living within a budget. This enables you to regularly set aside a tithe and other offerings for God's work. As a result, you may be:
- working toward (or have already achieved) a debt-free lifestyle
- building a surplus
- working diligently to reduce expenditures
- adopting a regular pattern of saving and/or investing
- striving to find God's purpose for your life, and
- setting specific financial goals for the future.

Week 1, Day 2

Is there a new habit God would like you to add? If so, write it here.

_____

_____

_____

Now be a little more specific. State some ways that you believe you are making yourself available to God's work now, more than ever before, because of a lifestyle change in the area of finances. *(Example: My wife and I now have a commitment to world hunger relief. Each payday we contribute $5.00 from our "dining-out" allocation to our hunger jar. Every three months we donate this money.)*

_____

_____

_____

If you are already flexing your muscles in areas like this, then making genuine sacrifice, as God prompts you, is simply the next step for you. Remember that sacrifice involves giving at some cost to you — giving until it hurts, sometimes. It involves laying it all down for Jesus' sake. See 1 John 3:16-18 at right.

One family I know believed Jesus was drawing great numbers of unsaved persons to attend their church. They saw that current facilities could not house the larger congregation, and they wanted to help enlarge its building. The family originally had planned a garage sale to raise funds for buying some outdoor furniture for their home. But they sensed Jesus telling them to give the money to the church building fund instead of keeping it for their own wants. They were willing to sacrifice for Jesus.

If you've been asking yourself "How much is enough?" then people, not things, have grown more important to you. If you've come to understand that your identity is not in possessions or achievements, then you want others to experience the same joy of knowing Jesus' unconditional love. If you now ask yourself, "What would Jesus do?" before you make any purchase or commit to any task, then Jesus is truly becoming Lord of all your life, and

"This is how we know what love is: Jesus Christ laid down his life for us. And we ought to lay down our lives for our brothers. If anyone has material possessions and sees his brother in need but has no pity on him, how can the love of God be in him? Dear children, let us not love with words or tongue but with actions and in truth."

–1 John 3:16-18

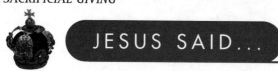

A SACRIFICIAL LIFESTYLE *continued . . .*

Scripture Verses

"And my God will meet all your needs according to his glorious riches in Christ Jesus."
–Philippians 4:19

healthy patterns are becoming ingrained. At this point, giving yourself over to true sacrifice will be as much a part of your lifestyle as your next breath.

How do you feel when you realize that you, indeed, may be well-equipped to sacrifice?

❑   I wonder if I could be as unselfish as the people in these examples are.
❑   I've tried something like this before, and it didn't last. Other needs or desires got in the way.
❑   I sincerely would like to lead a sacrificial life, but my patterns are so ingrained I worry that I can't change.
❑   I realize that on my own power I can't give until it hurts, but through Christ's power I can be this kind of mature follower.

I hope you were able to check the last statement. Only when you recognize that Jesus working through you is the only source of your power are you able to sacrifice.

Pray about this. Regardless of which answer you checked, be honest about this situation before God. Ask Him to enlarge your faith to help you with this challenging task. Write a brief prayer expressing your thoughts.

_____
_____
_____
_____
_____
_____
_____
_____

Week 1, Day 2

Notes

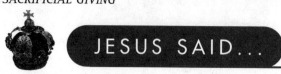

JESUS SAID...

Week 1, Day 3

A CAREFUL BALANCE

Scripture Verses

"If anyone does not provide for his relatives, and especially for his immediate family, he has denied the faith and is worse than an unbeliever."
                –1 Timothy 5:8

"But Ruth replied, 'Don't urge me to leave you or to turn back from you. Where you go I will go, and where you stay I will stay. Your people will be my people and your God my God.'"
                –Ruth 1:16-17

A natural response as you consider giving sacrificially is this: "I understand that Jesus is calling me to sacrifice. But what about my own family's needs? I don't want to deprive my loved ones as I look around for someone else to help."

No doubt, Christians would be tremendously negligent for turning blind eyes to family needs in order to help less fortunate outsiders. Parents who fail to take their sick children to the doctor or to buy new shoes when old ones are outgrown would be highly neglectful if they were, at the same time, giving huge sums of money to the local food bank or other types of community outreach.

The same thing applies to adults who allow their elderly parents to live in squalor while they spend thousands of dollars on church building funds. This is not the type of sacrifice God intends. Read at left what the Word says in 1 Timothy 5:8.

Likewise, the church member who spends every night of the week witnessing while neglecting family time is sidestepping his or her family responsibility.

Part of your Christian stewardship is proper care and nurture of your family — your spouse, your children, and other relatives, such as parents and grandparents (even in-laws; remember the story of Ruth and Naomi; see the passage at left.) To turn your back on those closest to you while you look all over the world for people to help is dereliction of duty. A Christ-honoring home and family life makes a lasting impression on its members and can be used by the Holy Spirit as an outreach to others.

One way to look at proper family care is like this: "If I take care of my family, someone else won't have to. Welfare systems won't have to; the government won't have to. Those tax dollars won't have to be used in wrong places. They can be spent to help the truly needy and destitute of the world."

That's why you've been spending this intense amount of time during your *Jesus On Money* study learning to discipline yourself to ask the question,

Week I, Day 3

Scripture Verses

"How much is enough?" — and not just in the area of finances. To see where the balance scales may need to be shifted, you've been asked to review every area of your life and examine your commitment of time, energies, and money. You've also been learning new, healthy patterns of managing your personal resources that will enable you to provide for your family in a way that honors Jesus.

State one way that you believe you are now providing more responsibly for your family as a result of something you've learned in *Jesus On Money*.

_____

_____

_____

Let's look at some places where Jesus taught specifically about this careful balance of where you are to put your attentions. One of the most obvious is the story of the Lord's visit to the home of Mary and Martha, when Mary sat at His feet to listen as He taught. That distressed Martha, who was apparently trying to impress Him with her activities. If you could have listened to the thoughts going on inside Martha's head, you might have heard her say something like this: "I'd like to stop what I'm doing and listen to Jesus. But if I don't prepare this food, my family, as well as our guest, may go hungry. How can I sacrifice my family's needs?"

When Martha then asked Jesus to rebuke Mary, His reply would fit most of us today. See Luke 10:41-42 at right.

If you had been in Martha's shoes, what might you have done to take care of the "one thing" that was needed without neglecting your family?

_____

_____

_____

Possibly Martha was overly attentive in her domestic preparations. Do you think her family and guest *really* would have gone hungry if she had sat at

"'Martha, Martha,' the Lord answered, 'you are worried and upset about many things, but only one thing is needed. Mary has chosen what is better, and it will not be taken away from her.'"
–Luke 10:41-42

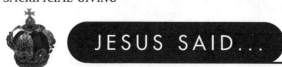

JESUS SAID...

Week 1, Day 3

A CAREFUL BALANCE *continued . . .*

Jesus' feet for a while? Perhaps the basic food needs were already covered and she was going overboard, to the point of distraction, and keeping herself from experiencing important spiritual food. Sometimes you view sacrificing as harsh deprivation when, in truth, you are caught up in the desire to keep doing more and more for your family — far beyond the point of meeting the basics necessary to life.

Is this the case with you? Do you use the excuse of "my family comes first" to avoid helping someone in more urgent need, even though the basics of life are already covered? If so, give an example below.

_____
_____
_____
_____

In the Mary/Martha story, Jesus states, "only one thing is needed" and goes on to describe it as a "better" thing. He affirms that the better thing that Mary has chosen, seeking His kingdom first, "will not be taken away from her." The choice that Mary makes in this story has eternal value.

What is Jesus saying to you as a modern day Martha?

_____
_____
_____
_____

These are weighty matters you're being asked to consider. For your prayer time, change the scenery. Take a walk, go for a drive in the country, or find a quiet place outdoors or in some other room of your home to meditate. Ask God to impress on you what He wants you to take away from this lesson today.

Week 1, Day 3

Notes

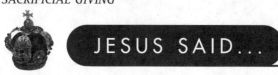

Week 1, Day 4

PLACE GOD'S KINGDOM FIRST

Scripture Verses

"If anyone comes to me and does not hate his father and mother, his wife and children, his brothers and sisters — yes, even his own life — he cannot be my disciple."
–Luke 14:26

"I have set you an example that you should do as I have done for you."
–John 13:15

"Anyone who loves his father or mother more than me is not worthy of me; anyone who loves his son or daughter more than me is not worthy of me; and anyone who does not take his cross and follow me is not worthy of me."
–Matthew 10:37-38

In Luke 14:16-26, Jesus told His disciples a parable about being a part of the kingdom of God. Many will be called to serve in God's kingdom, but most will have excuses why they can't get involved. At the conclusion of this parable is one of the most convicting Scriptures in all of Jesus' teachings. Read Luke 14:26 at left. Anyone who doubts the emphasis Jesus puts on placing His kingdom first, even before family and one's own life, should ponder that Scripture for a while.

Are there aspects of your life that consistently get in the way of your service to God? Describe here.

_____
_____
_____
_____
_____

Jesus is to be the most exalted being in God's eternal kingdom, although He assumed the lowliest, most humble position possible during His life. He not only served others, He also assumed the position of a foot-washer. See what Jesus said about this in John 13:15 at left. Perhaps this will mean giving up the most and the best for someone else.

Nothing comes before Jesus in the life of a disciple. See Matthew 10:37-38 in the margin. Ultimate loyalty can be given only to Him — not to husband, wife, children, or parents. Christian commitment includes faithful service to family, but Jesus must be supreme. Only one question determines if you are a disciple: Have you, in faith, given up everything for Him?

A man about to be appointed as a missionary to Asia left his career in a Fortune 500 company to go overseas. If he and his wife had waited only two more years, it would have meant a significantly larger amount for his retirement benefits. He pondered the value of this added money to his family but decided that following God's will immediately to take the gospel to those who had never heard was more important than more money.

Week 1, Day 4

I once met a Chinese Christian who was saved while he was a member of the Red Brigade in Communist China. He was imprisoned, tortured, starved, and beaten in an effort to get him to renounce his faith. When he refused, his family was executed to "teach others a lesson." He said he was sustained only by an ever-deepening relationship with Jesus and an unyielding commitment to serving God.

I have read and reread Paul's letter to the Romans. Paul describes himself as a man who accepts God as the absolute authority in his life and is willing to surrender everything, if necessary, to serve Him — even to the point of death. Paul had learned, as he expressed in Philippians 1:21, that you live to serve Christ at any cost, even if death is what you pay. See what Jesus said about this in John 15:13.

Perhaps God hasn't called you to the physical sacrifices that many Christians have suffered. But the admonition that Jesus gives to you is clear. See Matthew 6:25 at right. Compared to eternity, we are all dying tomorrow. Don't be so concerned for yourself and for your family that you forget the better thing, as Jesus told Martha.

You won't always reap the rewards immediately. In fact, I believe it is your choice whether to take what you want now or store it and receive it in God's eternal kingdom. When you compare the time to enjoy God's rewards to time spent in this world, there is no contest. See what Jesus said in Luke 18 at right.

Call your prayer partner. Ask that person to pray that you will have the courage to sacrifice whatever God asks of you, even if it means hardship or deprivation for the cause of Christ.

Scripture Verses

"For to me, to live is Christ and to die is gain."
–Philippians 1:21

"Greater love has no one than this, that he lay down his life for his friends."
–John 15:13

"For this reason I say to you, do not be anxious for your life, as to what you shall eat, or what you shall drink; nor for your body, as to what you shall put on. Is not life more than food, and the body than clothing?"
–Matthew 6:25, NASB

"And He said to them, 'Truly I say to you, there is no one who has left house or wife or brothers or parents or children, for the sake of the kingdom of God, who shall not receive many times as much at this time and in the age to come, eternal life.'"
–Luke 18:29-30, NASB

JESUS SAID...

THE RIGHT ATTITUDE

This Week

Scripture Verses

"If you had known what these words mean, 'I desire mercy, not sacrifice,' you would not have condemned the innocent."
–Matthew 12:7

Some wrongful attitudes can surface when a person considers sacrificing for Jesus. One very harmful attitude is that of egotism.

One believer working in full-time Christian ministry was so committed to serving others that he dedicated himself and his family to a life of extreme poverty. He believed that in order to serve Jesus a person must relinquish all ownership of worldly goods and "look poor." He sold his family's home, furniture, and numerous other possessions. He based this on what Jesus said in Luke 9:3: "He told them: 'Take nothing for the journey — no staff, no bag, no bread, no money, no extra tunic.'"

In this Scripture, Jesus taught His disciples a simple truth: trust God — He is sufficient. Jesus was directing His disciples to live by faith; those to whom they were ministering would supply their needs. No doubt Jesus has since directed others to do the same. However, I observe that one thing distinguishes those God chooses for such hardships: an attitude of peace and joy.

That certainly was not the case with the individual I met. He was egotistical about his commitment and openly critical of other Christians who lived what he called "carnal, worldly" lives. He also had open rebellion in his home — and understandably so. Each time his family made even the slightest material request, the man replied harshly, "God doesn't want us to have that." When I discussed the inconsistencies I saw in what he was doing, he rationalized them as sufferings for the Lord. I pointed out that the Pharisees of Jesus' day felt the same way.

The Pharisees did what they thought were great things for God. Most of the things they did were even the right things: they prayed, they fasted, they tithed. Jesus never challenged their actions; He challenged their motives. They were so blinded by their own self-righteousness they couldn't see God's true promises. He confronted them with this truth in Matthew 12:7 at left. Some were prideful in their poverty; others required the best of everything. In God's eyes, they suffered from a common malady: ego.

God calls each of us to a radical lifestyle of total commitment to Him, but rarely does Jesus call one of His own to voluntary poverty. If He does, He

Week 1, Day 5

fills that person with love, humility, and the acceptance that not everyone is called to sacrifice similarly.

The possession or absence of material things is not the question in serving Jesus; the attitude about them is. God knows what each person is called to do in the area of sacrifice, and He equips each to do it. In the case of this Christian, a major attitude change clearly would be needed before he could decide to suffer for Jesus in this way. Sacrificial giving with a right attitude is possible *only* for Christians who are totally submitted to God.

How do you respond to this story about the "suffering" Christian worker? Have you ever had a wrong attitude toward Christians you believed weren't giving enough or doing enough for the Lord? If so, describe here.

_____
_____
_____
_____
_____

You also can sacrifice with a wrong attitude when you show off or flaunt your sacrifice before others. This too is not biblical. The widow who gave her two small copper coins (Luke 21) wasn't giving to impress. The Temple didn't need her pennies, for it was plated with gold and brass. She gave all she had because she loved God and clearly felt a bigger need than that of food. She felt the need to sacrifice for God. Your stewardship is measured by the sacrifice you make, not by the amount you give or by others' reaction to it.

Does this challenge you? Have you ever sacrificed to impress others? If so, describe here.

_____
_____
_____

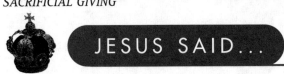

Week 1, Day 5

THE RIGHT ATTITUDE *continued . . .*

This Week

Scripture Verses

"Let each one do just as he has purposed in his heart; not grudgingly or under compulsion; for God loves a cheerful giver."

–2 Corinthians 9:7, NASB

A third harmful attitude occurs when you sacrifice but do so grudgingly and not cheerfully. Do you really think your sacrificial gift lays up eternal treasures for you when you give it while you grumble and complain? Do you really believe God doesn't hear your thoughts when you mutter to yourself, "Sure, I'll spend my afternoon helping my new neighbor unpack her moving boxes, but I really don't want to take time to do it." A reminder about this type of attitude appears in 2 Corinthians 9:7 at left. "Cheerful" is the operative word. I believe God would rather have no gift at all than one made with a bitter, grousing spirit.

We do not fully understand why God chooses to use people to carry out His purposes for the redemption of the world, but we know that He does. When we are unwilling to give what is needed for His work, He often simply distributes the necessary funds to Christians who have correct attitudes — primarily those who seek His will and are willing to sacrifice for the needs of others. If you, who are so mightily blessed, are not willing to sacrifice any of your desires for others, God may simply reallocate your supply to those who are.

Is that a heart-stopping thought to you? Perhaps God intends for it to be. Stop and pray about one specific sacrifice that God has placed on your heart during this week's study. Then write it below so you'll be less likely to forget how the Spirit has prompted you.

One thing I feel led to sacrifice for Jesus is _____

_____

_____

_____

Week 1, Day 5

Notes

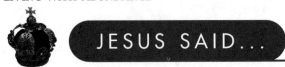

Week 2, Day 1

This Week

IDENTIFY YOUR ABUNDANCE

To the person struggling to survive from one paycheck to the next, the idea of managing a financial surplus may appear to be paradise! However, every lifestyle presents unique challenges to faithful stewardship, and managing abundance is no exception. Jesus said, "From everyone who has been given much, much will be demanded; and from the one who has been entrusted with much, much more will be asked" (Luke 12:48).

This week's daily studies will help you discover answers to difficult questions like, "How do I know when I have an abundance?" and "How much is enough?" You may wrestle with determining who deserves your support or whether you will give all your abundance to the church. The issue can become quite complicated.

Perhaps the greatest test of character and maturity is how you deal with your freedom . . . and your abundance of material goods! Given the opportunity to do as you please, will you choose to serve God or your own self-interests? It's a sobering question.

If God makes provision in your life beyond your needs, He has a reason. "At the present time your plenty will supply what they need, so that in turn their plenty will supply what you need. Then there will be equality, as it is written: 'He who gathered much did not have too much, and he who gathered little did not have too little'" (2 Corinthians 8:14). Have you organized your lifestyle and expenditures to create a surplus?

List any surplus you have seen as a result of lifestyle changes.

_____

_____

_____

_____

Remember when we discussed financial planning and living on a budget? The budget helped establish a surplus. If so, have you discovered God's plan for using this abundance? It is easy to slip away from God in your abundance.

Week 2, Day 1

List one need God has led you to meet from your abundance.

_____

_____

_____

Managing an abundance may be a daunting challenge, but the task provides a grand opportunity to demonstrate your love and faithfulness to Jesus Christ. To share from this surplus requires great love; it really means a greater love for God than money.

Likely, you are a person blessed by God with an abundance of material possessions. You may earn more money, have more possessions, and have access to more means with which to make more money than previous generations ever could have imagined. You probably are better educated and your children, if you are a parent, are likely to attend institutions of higher education. Even if your dwelling is modest, your house is still probably one that your ancestors a century ago could only have dreamed about, with modern conveniences that have swept you along at a faster and faster pace.

List two ways that you see yourself as more materially prosperous than your grandparents were.

1. _____
2. _____

Your church, like most today, is probably larger, better equipped, and more prosperous than ever before. Churches the size of St. Peter's in Rome, once considered the consummate in church size, dot the landscape across America today. Even small congregations often have facilities that would have been highly appreciated by worshippers of past generations.

List two ways that you believe your church is more prosperous than it was five or even ten years ago.

1. _____
2. _____

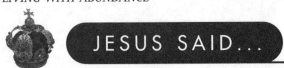

JESUS SAID...

Week 2, Day 1

This Week

Scripture Verses

"The thief comes only to steal and kill and destroy; I have come that they may have life, and have it to the full."
–John 10:10

"The grace of our Lord was poured out on me abundantly, along with the faith and love that are in Christ Jesus."
–1 Timothy 1:14

IDENTIFY YOUR ABUNDANCE *continued . . .*

Why do you think you have prospered? "Because I am so deserving," you might say. Others might surmise that this prosperity has occurred because Christians have followed biblical principles for living and investing. Some might say the so-called Protestant work ethic, mixed with frugality and the blessings of God on our nation, was proved right once again.

All of those answers are correct in some ways. Diligent work and careful management do pay off long-term. Following biblical guidelines on debt and spending practices is important. But let me suggest an even better answer: *You have been blessed with abundance in order to bless others.* Read Psalm 67.

I'm not suggesting that you give everything away to the poor and become poor again yourself. And *Jesus On Money* is not designed to convince you that you are rich by comparing you with some poor person living in rural Honduras. But I repeat that whatever blessings you can count, whether few or many, are given you for your stewardship. Part of that stewardship is passing on the blessing to others.

When you think of the word *abundance* as it relates to the Bible, you may automatically think of Scriptures that speak about abundant life in Christ and other spiritual blessings. See two of those verses in the margin.

Although I want to focus on abundant living spiritually, a study of the Scriptures finds God again and again speaking about the abundance of material blessings: cattle, oxen, harvest, and other possessions as well. The Bible speaks of the Promised Land as abounding with good things to eat and the potential for wealth.

Read the verses from 1 Kings and 1 Chronicles appearing in the far right margin. Underline some of the references to physical abundance.

Clearly the people of God sometimes could not see their abundance because their wants and desires were in their way. But these verses confirm that they really had an abundance of physical blessings.

Week 2, Day 1

When God called Abraham (Genesis 12:1-3) to leave his home and resettle in the Promised Land, God promised, "I will make you into a great nation and I will bless you. I will make your name great, and you will be a blessing . . . and all peoples on earth will be blessed through you."

Abraham was promised material blessings, and the Scriptures say that he received these. His flocks and herds grew in number, his tents were enlarged, his possessions were expanded, and he was truly thought of as a prosperous man. But he was blessed not to be able to brag, "Look how rich I am," but in order to bless others.

When Abraham and his nephew Lot decided to split their herds and possessions, he generously asked Lot which of the lands he preferred. Abraham wasn't greedy. He wanted to bless Lot also.

But God's greater purpose in blessing Abraham was not in just blessing Lot or others in Abraham's family materially. God blessed and raised up Abraham in order that, through Abraham, God would be able to reach out to others spiritually for generations to come.

Fill in the following chart. (*Example: My automobile — I can use it to take my handicapped neighbor to doctor visits. My house — I can use it to hold Bible studies.*)

Ways I have been blessed:	Ways I can use that blessing to bless others:
_____	_____
_____	_____
_____	_____
_____	_____
_____	_____

As you pray to conclude today's work, ask God to help you count your blessings. Ask Him to remind you to truly demonstrate your love for Him and not to keep His benefits to yourself.

"And she gave the king 120 talents of gold, large quantities of spices, and precious stones. Never again were so many spices brought in as those the queen of Sheba gave to King Solomon."
–1 Kings 10:10

"I have taken great pains to provide for the temple of the Lord a hundred thousand talents of gold, a million talents of silver, quantities of bronze and iron too great to be weighed, and wood and stone. And you may add to them."
–1 Chronicles 22:14

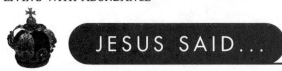

JESUS SAID...

Week 2, Day 2

MORE ABUNDANCE IN THE BIBLE

This Week

Scripture Verses

"For two years now there has been famine in the land, and for the next five years there will not be plowing and reaping. But God sent me ahead of you to preserve for you a remnant on earth and to save your lives by a great deliverance."
          –Genesis 45:6-7

" . . . Walk in his ways, and keep his decrees and commands, his laws and requirements, as written in the Law of Moses, so that you may prosper in all you do and wherever you go, and that the Lord may keep his promise to

continued in right margin . . .

T he Bible is full of additional stories, besides that of Abraham, of people whom God blessed so they could bless others.

Read the passage at left that tells about Joseph's prosperity in Egypt. Why does it say God prospered Joseph?

_____

_____

_____

Joseph prospered in Egypt not for his own glory nor to demonstrate his skill but that through his prosperity he would be able to save the people, deliver his starving family, be reconciled with his brothers, and fulfill God's plans for his family and his life.

When King David was near death, he pronounced a blessing on his son, Solomon. See the verses from 1 Kings which begin in the margin at left. David knew that faithfulness to God coupled with His blessings of prosperity would keep Solomon on the throne and would extend his reign and reach.

From what you know about the story of Ruth, after she married Boaz, how did she turn her prosperity into a blessing for others?

_____

_____

_____

When she married the respected Israelite farmer, Boaz, Ruth's life suddenly turned around from the insecure existence she had faced as a widow. In the material prosperity she no doubt enjoyed from this union, Ruth continued to bless her former mother-in-law, Naomi. In Ruth 4:15, the Bible describes Ruth as being "better to Naomi than seven sons." Ruth also went on to bless all peoples of the world by producing a son, Obed, from whose line Jesus would descend. God blessed this dedicated Moabite woman and then used her to carry out His saving purposes for the world.

From the examples of these Bible characters, you can continue to see that God intends for you to bless others with what you've been blessed with.

Week 2, Day 2

Scripture Verses

Besides these Old Testament stories, we can also focus on some New Testament admonitions.

In Luke 12:15, Jesus said, "Watch out! Be on your guard against all kinds of greed; a man's life does not consist in the abundance of his possessions."

Can you describe a time in which you may have thought that your life was valued by what you possessed? *(Example: I once thought all my clothes had to have designer labels in order to make me appear competent and capable.)*

_____
_____
_____
_____

In 2 Corinthians 8:1-4 Paul describes the Macedonian churches who gave generously even when they did not appear to have the resources for such gifts. See these verses in the margin.

Can you think of a time when you did as the Macedonian churches did — gave to bless others, when you did not have the resources to give? Tell about it here.

_____
_____
_____
_____

Paul says these churches not only gave but they *pleaded* to be able to do so. Think what your life and your ministry would be like if you found yourself literally begging for the ability to share with those whom God placed on your heart.

Stop and pray a prayer similar to this one: "Dear Lord, I confess I've not always viewed my blessings in this manner. Change my attitude, Lord. Amen."

me: 'If your descendants watch how they live, and if they walk faithfully before me with all their heart and soul, you will never fail to have a man on the throne of Israel.'"
–1 Kings 2:3b-4

"And now, brothers, we want you to know about the grace that God has given the Macedonian churches. Out of the most severe trial, their overflowing joy and their extreme poverty welled up in rich generosity. For I testify that they gave as much as they were able, and even beyond their ability. Entirely on their own, they urgently pleaded with us for the privilege of sharing in this service to the saints."
–2 Corinthians 8:1-4

JESUS SAID...

Week 2, Day 3

Scripture Verses

"Give proper recognition to those widows who are really in need."
–1 Timothy 5:3

WHO DESERVES MY HELP?

Perhaps by now you've become convinced that you truly have an abundance (or plan to create one), and you desire to share it. But where? How can you do this confidently? Who is deserving, and why? Do you give all your abundance to the church, or do other causes merit support?

As we discuss this topic, I'm going to assume that you already are giving your tithe (10 percent) to God's work. When I talk about abundance, I mean gifts above and beyond the tithe.

Certainly the Bible indicates that you are to care for the Christian community. In 1 Timothy 5:3, Paul directs the church to honor "widows who are really in need" — persons who have no family to support them. In such cases, the burden of support is placed on the church; the church is to supply their needs.

How many churches really do that today? How many congregations in the United States have, as a regular part of their budgets, money to supply the needs of Christians in their churches who cannot make their own way? This includes those who are temporarily out of work, the injured or disabled, the elderly, or those who are so emotionally paralyzed that they cannot support themselves.

In God's plan, the church is to distribute His money to the needs of the body. Galatians 6:10 says that you are to "do good to all people, especially to those who belong to the family of believers." Unfortunately, not all churches adhere to this plan. I believe that if a church observes God's plan, both in teaching His Word and administering His money, then your money — both your tithe *and* your abundance — can safely be placed in its care.

No doubt virtually every congregation has, at some time, experienced the abuse or unwise management of benevolence funds. As a result, many churches have grown indifferent and overly protective in this area. In reality, the answer in this vital area is better planning, wiser management, and more realistic goals. Jesus told us, "By this all men will know that you are my disciples, if you love one another" (John 13:35).

Week 2, Day 3

The church, as the individual, is confronted with a basic choice: will it be a "doer" or merely a "hearer" of the Word? Under no circumstances can the qualified needy be ignored. See in the margin what Jesus said about this to the Pharisees in Matthew 15:5-6.

If your church does not understand God's plan, work diligently to help it do so and remember there is specific accountability for being faithful in this stewardship area.

Do you know how your church ministers to people in need in your congregation? ❏ Yes ❏ No

What procedure does your church follow to help people with food, shelter, or medical needs?

_____
_____
_____
_____

_____
_____

You are also directed to share with the non-Christian community. When God talks specifically about the "believer," the "elect," or the "body of Christ," He refers to Christians. Other Scriptures that deal with sharing but do not refer directly to the body of Christ are intended to include the non-Christian community.

I have found that the majority of Scripture deals with supplying the needs of the non-Christian community. Perhaps 10 times as many references pertain to sharing with unbelievers. Study what Jesus says in Matthew 5:42 and 10:42 at right.

Neither of those Scriptures, as well as more than 50 others, deals only with Christians. They deal with the community at large — both believers and unbelievers.

Scripture Verses

"But you say that if a man says to his father or mother, 'Whatever help you might otherwise have received from me is a gift devoted to God,' he is not to 'honor his father' with it. Thus you nullify the word of God for the sake of your tradition."
–Matthew 15:5-6

"Give to the one who asks you, and do not turn away from the one who wants to borrow from you."
–Matthew 5:42

"And if anyone gives even a cup of cold water to one of these little ones because he is my disciple, I tell you the truth, he will certainly not lose his reward."
–Matthew 10:42

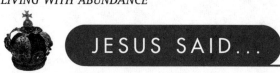

WHO DESERVES MY HELP? *continued . . .*

This Week

Day 1: Identify Your Abundance
Day 2: More Abundance in the Bible
Day 3: Who Deserves My Help?
Day 4: Evaluate the Recipient
Day 5: Give Jesus

Scripture Verses

"Sell your possessions and give to the poor. Provide purses for yourselves that will not wear out, a treasure in heaven that will not be exhausted, where no thief comes near and no moth destroys."
–Luke 12:33

You are to witness to non-Christians through your material resources. As you do so, you demonstrate that Christ, not money, rules your life. Commitment in Christianity is often related to whether one is more committed to money than to the needs of others. Jesus based much of His teaching on this principle. See Luke 12:33 at left.

For example, I know a businessman and his wife who use their abundance to reach out to internationals in their community. They routinely invite new immigrants to dinner and provide them with Bibles in their native language as they hopefully lay the groundwork for witnessing opportunities. I also know doctors who give up their vacation time and personal funds to provide free medical care for people in poverty-stricken areas, both inside and outside the United States. I know a mother of five who routinely makes and delivers casseroles or desserts to newcomers in her neighborhood, regardless of their religious affiliation.

Can you name something you've done recently in which you've reached out materially to aid a nonbeliever? *(Example: I donated a baby crib to a crisis pregnancy center, where the majority of young women served are not Christians.)*

_____

_____

_____

_____

_____

_____

Ask God to place on your heart a nonbeliever who needs your physical assistance. Trust God to give you the ability to meet that need.

Week 2, Day 3

Notes

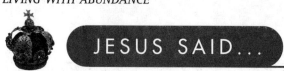

Week 2, Day 4

EVALUATE THE RECIPIENT

This Week

Scripture Verses

"The integrity of the upright will guide them, But the falseness of the treacherous will destroy them."
  –Proverbs 11:3, NASB

"Instruct a wise man and he will be wiser still; teach a righteous man and he will add to his learning."
  –Proverbs 9:9

When helping people or organizations, two questions arise.
  1. Does the recipient use the money in a godly manner?
  2. How do I know which organizations deserve my support?
  Be highly sensitive, not only concerning those whom you assist but how the recipient uses your money. See Proverbs 11:3 at left.

Describe what guidelines you have used to determine this in the past for groups or persons to which you have given.

_____

_____

_____

The standards are clear for individuals: Assess whether they are willing and able to work. Also, are they asking for needs or for wants and desires? Get personally involved with the people you help, if possible. Share God's principles of finance with them. Help them establish a budget and live by it. Find out how they are living. Are they wasting their present income in foolishness? If so, you have no requirement to support them. In fact, by doing so, you may well be interfering in God's plan for them.

For example, people who waste their income on the abuse of alcohol may need to experience the logical consequences of their actions if they are ever to begin recovery. God's plan for an alcohol abuser may be that he or she actually loses his or her job and becomes destitute for a while in order to be confronted with harmful behavior. If you give that person handouts of money, it may prolong the time in which he or she faces the reality of all that was lost because of drinking.

Gary was a Christian single dad who struggled to support his three young children on a mechanic's wages. Ralph, a friend in his church, wanted to help. Instead of giving Gary cash donations, Ralph arranged for him to regularly work on his cars. He gave toys and books to Gary's children. Ralph also recruited Gary to attend some financial planning classes that he taught in his church as a layperson. These situations gave Ralph the opportunity to observe how Gary managed his resources. After some time, Gary opened his own automotive shop and got back on his feet for keeps. See the verse at left.

Week 2, Day 4

Scripture Verses

Have you ever helped someone financially? Describe your experience here. How did you determine that the person could be trusted with God's wealth as it was given through you?

_____

_____

_____

_____

What about the organizations approaching you? How can you assess whether they are doing God's work? Assess Christian organizations with discretion too. Today Christians are besieged by charitable requests from every side. Many groups are deserving, but some are poorly managed, unfruitful, and even dishonest. Seek God's wisdom before you give. Obtain literature that thoroughly describes the organization and its doctrine. Talk to others who have invested. Require references if you have not heard of the group before. Let the organization know why you are questioning its management. Be discerning; be a good steward of God's resources. See the verse at right.

"Now it is required that those who have been given a trust must prove faithful."
–1 Corinthians 4:2

The following is a suggested checklist.
1. If the organization comes in the name of Christ, is it communicating the true message of Jesus Christ? If it is not, do not get involved with it. You would be better off to give through a reputable secular organization that does worthy charitable work.
2. In evaluating either Christian or secular organizations, determine whether people respond to the organization positively. Are lives being changed as a result of the group's work?
3. Is the organization seeking and accomplishing goals? How does this occur? Any worthy organization can eagerly explain its goals to you.
4. Are the lives of those in leadership positions consistent with scriptural principles? Remember that many leaders of secular organizations are also devoted Christians who seek to carry out Jesus' commands in the secular realm.
5. Is the organization multiplying itself, or is it dying? Ask around, and be discerning. Pay a visit to the organization personally, particularly if your decision involves a large amount of money.

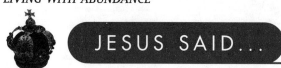

Week 2, Day 4

This Week

EVALUATE THE RECIPIENT *continued . . .*

6. Does a standard of excellence exist alongside a freedom from lavishness and waste? How much does the group spend to raise money? If you find an organization that spends one-fourth or more of its finances in order to raise more money, question its effectiveness. Can you invest elsewhere and get a better return for God's money?

7. Check out the group with other Christian organizations. If you feel led to give through a well-intentioned secular group, investigate it among similar organizations in your community. Explain that you are looking for honest answers about the group's effectiveness.

Go back and put a star by any of these suggestions that you have tried before in assessing where to make a donation. Be prepared to explain your experience to your group.

Share willingly according to God's plan, but be wise and cautious as a steward. Accept nothing less than excellence for the Lord's money.

Write a prayer, asking God's help as you give wisely. If you have been less than cautious in the past, ask for God's forgiveness. Ask Him to help you view the situation through His eyes.

_____

_____

_____

_____

_____

_____

_____

_____

_____

Week 2, Day 4

Notes

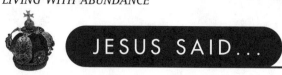

GIVE JESUS

This Week

Day 1:   Identify Your Abundance
Day 2:   More Abundance in the Bible
Day 3:   Who Deserves My Help?
Day 4:   Evaluate the Recipient
Day 5:   Give Jesus

Scripture Verses

" . . . (Jesus is) the Lamb of God, who takes away the sin of the world!"
                —*John 1:29b*

As you think about giving, the gift of Jesus is the greatest gift of all. See the verse at left. I will conclude this week's work by proposing one additional means for sharing your abundance. You've probably heard the expression, "Give a man a fish and he'll eat for one day; teach him to fish and he'll eat for a lifetime." Christians can follow Jesus' teaching and provide for those less fortunate, but they can also do so in a way that the recipients learn to "fish" and won't go hungry the rest of their lives.

In John 4:13, Jesus said, "Whoever drinks of this water that I give him will never thirst." Jesus quenches our spiritual thirst for meaning and thus represents life at its richest and fullest — the abundant life mentioned in the Scripture that began this week's work. If you truly want to help someone in need, introduce that person to Jesus.

The FAITH Sunday School Evangelism Strategy offers an excellent tool for you to use in the process of sharing the good news of Christ with others. This strategy will engage you not only in learning to share your faith effectively with others, but it will place you in ongoing opportunities to do so. The idea is to make sharing the gift of the gospel a lifestyle for you individually and also for your Sunday School class. By operating through your Sunday School class or department, FAITH encourages you and a team of others from your class in making a personal investment in people that will produce an eternal legacy.

Consider how God multiplies the blessing of your obedience to His Great Commission! One person is blessed because he hears about God's love and provision of eternal life. This person receives that good news from a group of people (including you) who will receive him and nurture him in a Bible study group. You and your Sunday School class receive a new brother or sister in Christ. You also enjoy a stronger sense of fellowship and a keen awareness of the presence of the Holy Spirit in your lives. The kingdom of God grows; your church and your Sunday School grow; your faith grows; and the mission of Christ expands. What a legacy! (To learn more about FAITH call 1-877-324-8498 or check out www.lifeway.com/sundayschool/faith on the Internet.)

At each of their bimonthly meetings, International Mission Board (IMB) trustees hear a report on an individual or a couple who leave all or portions of

Week 2, Day 5

their estates for overseas missions work. What is surprising about these gifts is that most of the donors are not known in their communities as people of abundance. Yet, their gifts, collectively, create a pool of resources that allows the IMB to send hundreds of missionaries each year who could not be sent using traditional contributions. Some of these total several thousands of dollars. For example, a check for more than $900,000 arrived from the estate of a person who invested quietly and carefully over the years in order to share Jesus overseas for years to come.

I know countless people who drive around in 10-year-old cars to avoid debt and create a surplus so they can go with their church on missions trips to Latin American countries. Given the choice of spending $1,000 on a week-long trip to build houses, assist in a medical center, and witness to people who desperately need Jesus, they gladly choose the missions trip over new automobiles.

Have you ever directly set aside some "creature comforts" and, instead, given that money to a missions cause? If so describe it here.

_____

_____

An abundance can be found for such purposes if you first focus your eyes on your objective. Don't wait until you have $1 million in the bank to begin sharing that abundance!

Even churches are beginning to ask similar questions: What percentage of our budget do we spend on constructing larger, showier buildings, and what percentage do we spend sending our people to parts of the world where the gospel needs to be preached? One small, expanding church I know definitely needs more meeting space, but members voted to figure out ways to live within their current structure by meeting in nearby homes and renting a nearby community facility for educational space. At the same time, they were able to pay one-half of the cost of missions trips overseas for their members.

Do you know if your church has made a similar decision to cut back in some areas in order to promote missions causes? If so, be prepared to tell your group about it. Read the verse at right.

"As he approached Jerusalem and saw the city, he wept over it and said, 'If you, even you, had only known on this day what would bring you peace — but now it is hidden from your eyes.'"

–Luke 19:41

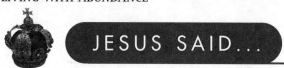

Week 2, Day 5

This Week

GIVE JESUS *continued . . .*

The opportunities are limitless. More than 1.7 billion people live in the Last Frontier, identified by evangelical missions agencies as that part of the world where the gospel has truly never been preached.

If Central Asia and the former Soviet republics don't appeal to you, Central America teems with people who will literally stand in line to ask the question of an American, "What must I do to be saved?" Even within our own shores, millions upon millions are caught in the throes of sin and godless existence. These are not only the addicts and prisoners and those you traditionally think of in need of Christ. America today is brimming with immigrants who come from these Last Frontier countries as well as others — immigrants who have never heard the gospel.

One of the most interesting and challenging ministries today is work with people who have left their native land for a freer life elsewhere. America is one of many countries to which these people move. Thanks to modern travel, these people often return to their native lands for a few weeks or months every year or so. Winning them to Christ has proved one of the best ways to introduce the gospel into closed countries where foreign missionaries would be barred.

You can witness to one of these immigrant families for the cost of a meal prepared and served in your own home, as I suggested in your Day-3 study.

Creative thinking will expand your horizons about how to invest your surplus. Practicing biblical principles for money management will help you create a surplus to spend on kingdom purposes. In God's creative hands your surplus can mushroom, as in Jesus' parable of the stewards and the talents. Hidden away, nothing grew. Creatively managed, God's blessings resulted.

Any donation to any physical cause, although worthy, brings only temporary results. Donating to the cause of the gospel gives people Jesus, the source of eternal life.

Week 2, Day 5

What has Jesus said to you this week? Briefly answer the following questions.

One way the Lord is leading me to create an abundance in my budget is

_____

_____

_____

One way God has blessed me that I had never thought about is

_____

_____

_____

One Christian or secular organization I believe the Lord is leading me to help with my resources is

_____

_____

_____

One way I will be personally involved in sharing Jesus is

_____

_____

_____

One way I want to challenge my church to do more to help needy believers is

_____

_____

_____

One way I intend to use my resources to give Jesus to those who need him is

_____

_____

_____

Week 3, Day 1

This Week

Scripture Verses

"The blessing of the Lord brings wealth, and he adds no trouble to it."
–Proverbs 10:22

"For we brought nothing into the world, and we can take nothing out of it. But if we have food and clothing, we will be content with that. People who want to get rich fall into temptation and a trap and into many foolish and harmful desires that plunge men into ruin and destruction. For the love of money is the root of all kinds of evil. Some people, eager for money, have wandered from the faith and pierced themselves with many griefs."
–1 Timothy 6:7-10

INSTANT RICHES

A contributing cause to discontentment in the Christian community is the failure to understand true wealth. The culture around you typically characterizes wealth by tangible things like new homes, jewelry, cars, or the size of an investment portfolio. By those terms, many people will never attain wealth.

In my counseling experience, however, I frequently discover people who are materially rich but spiritually poor. The material wealth becomes an albatross around their necks. It suffocates true joy and peace in life — quite the opposite of God's plan, which Proverbs 10:22 at left describes.

When describing wealth, however, the Bible includes many intangible measures, such as health, a steady job, fellowship in your church family, and true friends on which you can rely. Based on those factors, you certainly can be wealthy in this life, regardless of how much money you have in the bank. You may be wealthy right now and not know it!

A careful reading of 1 Timothy 6:7-10 (left margin) and 1 Timothy 6:17-18 (far right margin) indicates several cautions that God delivers to those who are wealthy, whether that wealth is tangible or intangible. Underline those cautions in the margin.

You may have underlined such phrases as "wandered from the faith," "plunge men into ruin and destruction," or "pierced themselves with many griefs."

This week's study will lead you to discover godly methods of dealing with wealth so that you can truly enjoy His provisions, strategically serve in His kingdom work, and retain peace and joy as well.

According to a story I read about John D. Rockefeller, Sr., one of the wealthiest men who ever lived, someone asked Rockefeller's accountant, "How much did John D. leave? We know he was immensely wealthy." The accountant answered, "Everything." Regardless of your station in life, you accumulate nothing. Wealth and possessions total zero at the moment of your death. Jesus reminds you not to "store up for yourselves treasures on earth" (Matthew 6:19-20).

Week 3, Day 1

Past civilizations show that wealth was often based on the number of cattle or camels owned, oil possessed, or many other material items. In the early U.S. economy, wealth was related to how much land one held. Later, wealth related to resources such as gold or silver or other natural elements in the earth. During the industrial revolution it related to how much a person had accumulated in worldly goods — namely, money.

In today's economy, wealth is still related to money, but position is also a measure of wealth. Professionals such as doctors, attorneys, dentists, and others are thought to be wealthy because of their income-earning potential. A doctor just out of residency can borrow great amounts of money to enter business with only his or her education as collateral. The doctor's credit is based on *potential productivity*. Therefore, even your talents and abilities are part of your wealth, as is your borrowing ability.

Name two of your skills or abilities on which you can rely to produce income or to provide for yourself and others. Then stop for a moment and thank God for giving this wealth to you.

_____

Depending on your attitude, wealth can be creative: You can use it to spread God's Word, build hospitals and churches, feed the poor, take care of orphans, or for many other activities. Or it can be wasted: spent on trivial pursuits, lavish living, gambling, or other destructive involvements. Wealth also can be corruptive: used to purchase influence, bribes, illegal business, or guns and bombs.

What is one way that you have personally misused some of the wealth (your time, talents, or possessions) God has entrusted to you? *(Example: I purchased a home that far exceeded my needs and went so heavily into debt that my family life suffered.)*

_____

_____

Scripture Verses

"Command those who are rich in this present world not to be arrogant nor to put their hope in wealth, which is so uncertain, but to put their hope in God, who richly provides us with everything for our enjoyment. Command them to do good, to be rich in good deeds, and to be generous and willing to share."
–1 Timothy 6:17-18

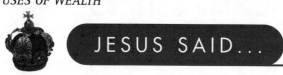

Week 3, Day 1

This Week

Scripture Verses

"Do not wear yourself out to get rich; have the wisdom to show restraint. Cast but a glance at riches, and they are gone, for they will surely sprout wings and fly off to the sky like an eagle."
    –Proverbs 23:4-5

" . . . in which you used to live when you followed the ways of this world and of the ruler of the kingdom of the air, the spirit who is now at work in those who are disobedient."
    –Ephesians 2:2

INSTANT RICHES *continued . . .*

For the Christian, wealth is what God entrusts to each of us. From the world's perspective, the creation of wealth revolves around many things, including how much self-control and willpower one has to devote to earning money. However, that is not God's perspective because, in every instance, individuals who spend their lives pursuing money end up frustrated and miserable. They never really understand why they have money. As they get closer to death, they realize the futility of attaining wealth. See Proverbs 23:4-5 at left.

The pursuit of gaining wealth is a poor investment of a life. First, it requires a great deal of time — to the virtual exclusion of everything else, including family, friends, spiritual growth, hobbies, and relaxation.

Can you recall a time in which your own pursuit of material items caused you to sacrifice more important areas, such as those mentioned above? If so, write about it here.

_____

_____

No correlation exists between wealth and happiness. Many Christians are inwardly disturbed by the prosperity of some non-Christians. Yet we recognize that Satan is the prince of this world, and it would be an extremely poor recruiting practice if he recruited only the impoverished! See Ephesians 2:2 at left.

A great difference exists between God and Satan in the area of your finances. Look back at Proverbs 10:22, on the first page of this week's study. This verse creates the foundation for the remainder of your study this week: how to have wealth without worry (wealth meaning your money, your creative abilities, everything you have acquired since you arrived on earth, and everything you will leave when you go).

Remember that wealth is temporary. The importance of wealth to God is that for this brief moment in time He wants you to use it to accomplish His eternal purposes. Your commitment to God's Word on this earth is directly related to your use of money.

Week 3, Day 1

See 2 Peter 3:11-12a at right. Underline the words that tell how God expects you to live, regardless of your possessions. Then, in prayer, ask Him to help you live this way.

Scripture Verses

"Since everything will be destroyed in this way, what kind of people ought you to be? You ought to live holy and godly lives as you look forward to the day of God and speed its coming."

–2 Peter 3:11-12a

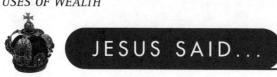

JESUS SAID...

Week 3, Day 2

ATTITUDES TOWARD WEALTH

Scripture Verses

" . . . so in Christ we who are many form one body, and each member belongs to all the others. We have different gifts, according to the grace given us. If a man's gift is prophesying, let him use it in proportion to his faith. If it is serving, let him serve; if it is teaching, let him teach; if it is encouraging, let him encourage; if it is contributing to the needs of others, let him give generously; if it is leadership, let him govern diligently; if it is showing mercy, let him do it cheerfully."
                 –Romans 12:5-8

W hat, then, is the correct attitude for you to have toward wealth? It is to seek God's purpose in what He supplies to you. The Christian can trust God in every circumstance. If you believe God really loves you and will give you only the amount of money, ability, or energy that you can deal with without worry, you can have perfect peace in finances.

As you've studied already, money is used as a training ground for God to develop and for you to discover your trustworthiness. Why do you, as a Christian, have trouble trusting God in this area? If you really don't believe that He will only do the best for you, you tend to want to withhold a part of what you have. But until you have experienced freedom from your wealth, you will never experience God's total plan for your life.

Let's look at some myths that exist about wealth, particularly in the religious realm, and consider what attitude God wants you to have.

Myth #1: Poverty is next to spirituality. Wrong. Dishonest poor exist, just as do dishonest rich. God never impoverished anyone to make them spiritual. Even in Job's case, God allowed his wealth to be removed as a testimony to God.

In the story of Job, what do you remember happened to Job when he stood true to God? (Job 42:10-17)

_____
_____
_____
_____

When Job demonstrated his allegiance to God, He returned Job's wealth twofold. God condemns the misuse or the preoccupation with money, not the money itself. In Scripture, God lists the production of money as a spiritual gift. Romans 12:5-8 at left describes the gift of giving. Obviously, if a gift of *giving* exists, a gift of *gathering* also must exist, as you cannot give otherwise. In every Scripture reference, the Word promises that as you give, you will be blessed.

Week 3, Day 2

Scripture Verses

Myth #2: Money brings happiness. Look back at 1 Timothy 6:17 in your Day-1 study. If riches could bring happiness, then the wealthy would be the most contented group of all. Instead, many frustrated, wealthy people exist. They are anxious about what they will do with their money, how they will leave it to their children, and what effect it will have. Many children fail to appreciate the large amounts of wealth their families leave them. Affluence can have a devastating effect on a family.

Can you think about a time when you thought, "If only I had money for ... I'd be truly happy," only to be disappointed when you finally realized your goal? If so, describe.

_____

_____

_____

_____

Myth #3: To be wealthy is a sin. That is false, too. Having a large amount of money is not a sin. Many times when God finds someone with the proper *attitude* He blesses that person with great riches. When God bestowed riches on Abraham, it was not His intention to corrupt the nation of Israel. When Solomon prayed for wisdom to be able to manage the people of Israel, God responded by granting him wisdom *and* great wealth. Psalm 8:6 says, "You made him ruler over the works of your hands." This represents God's stewardship to you over *everything* on earth.

Myth #4: Money is the root of all evil. Many people wrongly believe this misquote comes from Scripture. That is not what the Bible says. Paul points out in 1 Timothy 6:10, "For the *love* of money is a root of all sorts of evil, and some by longing for it have wandered away from the faith, and pierced themselves with many a pang" (NASB). Jesus relates this attitude to the rich young ruler (Luke 18:18-24 in the margin), about whom He comments, "How hard it is for the rich to enter the kingdom of God!" Jesus knew that, inside, this man loved money. He had kept all the external commandments, but he could not keep that internal attitude straight. Because of this, Jesus asked him to sell what he had and follow

"A certain ruler asked him, 'Good teacher, what must I do to inherit eternal life?' 'Why do you call me good?' Jesus answered. 'No one is good – except God alone. You know the commandments: do not commit adultery, do not murder, do not steal, do not give false testimony, honor your father and mother.' 'All these I have kept since I was a boy,' he said. When Jesus heard this, he said to him, 'You still lack one thing. Sell everything you have and give to the poor, and you will have treasure in heaven. Then come, follow me.' When he heard this, he became very sad, because he was a man of great wealth. Jesus looked at him and said, 'How hard it is for the rich to enter the kingdom of God!'"
–Luke 18:18-24

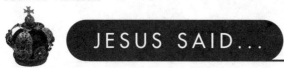

JESUS SAID...

This Week

ATTITUDES TOWARD WEALTH *continued . . .*

Him. The young man refused to do so; yet in his eventual death he surrendered what in life he could not.

Attitude is always God's concern. Jesus' comment about the rich young ruler's wealth was based on that man's attitude, his motivation, and the purpose behind his money. Riches do not shut the rich out of God's kingdom, but they do blind people to God's values.

What riches do you possess that dim your view of God's values? I'm not asking you to list them but just to think about them. Ask God to search your heart and show you how something you own or some ability you have has taken on so much importance that it blinds you to God. Ask Him to forgive you and to remove the blinders from your eyes.

Write a brief prayer of your intention to value what God values.

_____

_____

_____

_____

_____

_____

_____

Week 3, Day 2

Notes

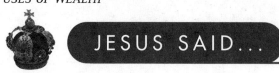

JESUS SAID...

Week 3, Day 3

Scripture Verses

"For the pagans run after all these things, and your heavenly Father knows that you need them. But seek first his kingdom and his righteousness, and all these things will be given to you as well."
    –Matthew 6:32-33

"If you, then, though you are evil, know how to give good gifts to your children, how much more will your Father in heaven give good gifts to those who ask him!"
        –Matthew 7:11

HOW GOD CAN WORK THROUGH RICHES

Your money can actually be the vehicle through which God works out His will. As you studied in Week 2, material blessings do not come to you by accident; everything you have is a gift from God. He intends for you to use all gifts for His glory and honor.

1. **God will use money to strengthen your trust in Him.** Often through money, God can clearly and objectively show you that He is God and is in control of everything. See what Jesus says in Matthew 6:32-33 in the left margin. This principle means that God will use money to strengthen your trust if you will just accept your position as steward and turn it over to Him.

Perhaps you have enough money to be comfortable now, but you may recall a time when you ran short — maybe were even impoverished. As you look back, what do you think God taught you about Himself in that circumstance?

_____
_____
_____
_____

2. **God will use money to develop your trustworthiness.** This principle is important because your life revolves around the making, spending, saving, and other uses of money. How trustworthy are you with what He provides? If you waste your resources and do not use them for the purposes for which He intends, why should He continue to give them to you? Remember what Jesus says in Luke 16:11, "If you have not been trustworthy in handling worldly wealth, who will trust you with true riches?"

3. **God will use money to prove His love.** Many Christians remain outside God's will because they are afraid to yield their lives and resources to Him. See Matthew 7:11 in the margin. Based on what Jesus says, you can see that God assumes the responsibility of providing good gifts to His children who trust Him.

Week 3, Day 3

Can you think of a time in which you withheld yielding your resources to God, out of fear that He would not continue to provide? If so, describe here.

_____

_____

_____

_____

Perhaps that time is right now. Before you go further in today's study, stop and ask God to examine your heart. Is fear causing you to withhold something of yourself that is rightfully His? If so, confess it to God and ask Him to remove that fear so you can be obedient to Him.

4. **God will use money to demonstrate His power over the world.** You may forget that you worship the Creator of the universe. We often think of God in human terms and relate to Him as we relate to human beings. Understanding God's power and His resources is vital.

Suppose that one day a man knocks on your door. When you answer, he says, "I've decided to give you $1,000 in two weeks." He then leaves you his card and shuts the door. You think, "Now, that was strange," but the first thing you do is to start checking him out. You want to find out what his bank balance is and how much money he's worth. You begin to talk to people around you who might know something about him.

You discover that he is a multi-billionaire and that he has given thousands of dollars to other people. Knowing this, your confidence in him grows. But still you don't have any real trust, because he has not given *you* any money. However, in two weeks, he delivers the $1,000. Your trust in him grows more. But, even while you rejoice in your good fortune, you still have some questions. Then, in another two weeks, he returns and says, "I've decided to give you $10,000 in two more weeks." You already know that he is a multi-billionaire, so you know he has the resources. In talking to other people, you discover that, sure enough, he has given away tens of thousand of dollars as well. This time, you discover something else: He never lies under any circumstances. When he says he's going to do something, he always does it.

JESUS SAID...

Week 3, Day 3

Scripture Verses

"For there is no difference between Jew and Gentile – the same Lord is Lord of all and richly blesses all who call on him."
    –Romans 10:12

" . . . He who gathered much did not have too much, and he who gathered little did not have too little."
    –2 Corinthians 8:15

HOW GOD CAN WORK THROUGH RICHES
continued . . .

In two weeks, he delivers $10,000. Now, your trust really grows. Over the next few months he continues to give you more and more money; each time your trust grows even more. So, with full confidence, you can actually spend that money, knowing that he will deliver exactly what he said.

Trust in God is similar. God makes promises to you through His Word, and within the pages of the Bible you will find everything God will ever do for you. As you read it, you begin to understand that God, indeed, owns everything. He is a multi-zillionaire; He is a multi-universaire! When He says He can supply things, He delivers.

Are you holding back on giving to God's work because you lack confidence that He will provide for you if you do? Even if you have ample money, you may wonder what will happen to you if you give generously. Remember, this is Creator God you're dealing with. He has all of the world's resources at His disposal, to provide for those who are faithful to Him. See Romans 10:12 in the margin.

5. **God will use money to unite Christians through many shared blessings.** See 2 Corinthians 8:15 at left. God will use the prosperity of one Christian to supply the needs of another. Later He may reverse the relationship, as 2 Corinthians 8:14 describes, "At the present time your plenty will supply what they need, so that in turn their plenty will supply what you need. Then there will be equality." Any surplus of money is in your life for a purpose.

For example, God sent Joseph into Egypt specifically to supply the needs of Israel. Had Joseph refused his position of stewardship, God simply would have assigned it to someone else.

What position of stewardship has He given you? Perhaps you began thinking about this during Week 2 as you studied abundance. Think of the name of a person or group for you to bless. Jot down names or initials here, along with your plan to bless that person.

_____

_____

_____

Week 3, Day 3

6. God uses money to provide direction for your life. No way exists for God to direct your life faster than through the abundance or lack of money. You may believe God directs your life only through plenty. However, through lack of money, God steers you down His path just as quickly. See Galatians 6:9 in the margin. God will ultimately supply the direction you seek. One of the primary ways He gives insight into His will is by providing or withholding money. Whichever economic strata they represent, Christians who seek God's will must be certain that they have first relinquished control of their lives, including the area of finances, and truly seek God's direction.

7. God uses money to satisfy the needs of others. Christians who hoard money and never plan to make giving a part of their lives cannot experience this area of fulfillment. Often I hear Christians say, "How can I give? I only have enough to barely meet my needs now."

Sometimes people keep making this statement long after they are financially prosperous and are well beyond the "barely-meeting-my-needs" stage. If you have never learned to give, God can never give back. God will not be in control as long as you believe you are the owner.

Glance back over the seven ways you just read about that God can work through riches. Put a star by the one(s) you need to experience the most growth in concerning how you view your material resources. Ask God to help you grow in this way.

Scripture Verses

"Let us not become weary in doing good, for at the proper time we will reap a harvest if we do not give up."
–Galatians 6:9

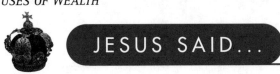

JESUS SAID...

Week 3, Day 4

Scripture Verses

"The heart of the discerning acquires knowledge; the ears of the wise seek it out."
        –Proverbs 18:15

"Then we will no longer be infants, tossed back and forth by the waves, and blown here and there by every wind of teaching and by the cunning and craftiness of men in their deceitful scheming."
        –Ephesians 4:14

WHY ACCUMULATE WEALTH?

Virtually everyone in America has the potential to accumulate a surplus. What you consider to be a minimum standard of living is significantly above what people experience in other parts of the world. Someone living on a small, fixed income has the possibility of accumulating tens of thousands of dollars through scrimping and sacrificing. With that potential, having godly reasons for accumulating money becomes vital.

Let's look at why you may accumulate money.

1. **Others advise it** — Many people get into investments, business, or other ventures simply because someone tells them to do so. They don't have any clear personal plans or goals. They simply commit their resources to some program because someone else thinks it's a good idea.

Read the verses at left from Proverbs and Ephesians. What do you think these passages say to you about receiving advice on how you amass your money?

_____
_____
_____
_____

Weigh everything against what Jesus says. Listen to new ideas, but do so prudently. Seek direction from the Word before you act. Get involved in an investment only because you believe it enhances your ministry and your family life and you feel a clear sense of peace about it.

2. **Envy of others** — Many people accumulate money simply because they envy others. They fall into the trap of "keeping up with the Joneses." Advertising promotes this attitude. You begin to allow those around you to dictate your lifestyle.

A man I know maintained a "follow-the-leader" attitude. He moved into a large home and bought new cars because his friends had them. By the time this man recognized he was in financial trouble, a new challenge appeared. A

Week 3, Day 4

Scripture Verses

friend was selling a new franchise product and dragged him into his get-rich-quick scheme. The man in my example had never sold anything in his life, but his envy overcame his hesitation. He borrowed money to begin the franchise, only to see losses when the scheme fell apart. He was a Christian, but he was ashamed to even talk about Christ because of his failures.

Read Luke 12:15 in the margin. Below, paraphrase what you think Jesus says about this type of "keeping-up-with-the-Joneses" lifestyle.

_____
_____
_____
_____

Have you ever, like the man I just mentioned, felt your ability to witness for Christ was diluted because your financial life made you a poor example? ❑ Yes ❑ No **If so, explain.**

_____
_____
_____
_____
_____

"Then he said to them, 'Watch out! Be on your guard against all kinds of greed; a man's life does not consist in the abundance of his possessions.'"

–Luke 12:15

3. **Game of it** — Many people accumulate money as a game; they match themselves against others relentlessly. The world system also promotes this concept. It elevates winners regardless of how they play the game.

"Walter Winner" started his gaming career early in life. He made it through college and into a profession. His work quickly bored him because competing against himself was no fun, so Walter began to diversify into investments and business. Soon he was well-known as an investor and a "wheeler-dealer." Although he wouldn't purposefully cheat anyone, he seemed to always come out on the high side. He gave to his church but not in proportion to what he received. He felt that giving more than he could write off in taxes was dumb. Nearly all of the money he earned was needed to expand his investment portfolio, he contended.

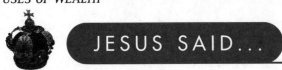

WHY ACCUMULATE WEALTH? *continued...*

The purpose of a game is to entertain, and non-Christians entertain themselves in the area of money. God does not provide this alternative for the Christian. Those who get involved with the game of making money are soon overcome by their pastime. They lose sight of their families because they are so involved with the game that everyone becomes a pawn.

One of the best ways to avoid this trap is through a long-range plan for surplus. Commit a large portion of each investment to the Lord's work. The results are predictable; a change in your attitude and perhaps even in the supply will occur. As Jesus speaks and you follow, He will transfer your ability from serving self to serving God.

Go back to the three reasons just mentioned that some people accumulate wealth. Underline any statements with which you can identify or which have applied to some of your motivations, either in the past or presently.

In your Day-5 study, you'll discover three additional wrongful reasons for amassing wealth. Then you'll study a godly reason.

Week 3, Day 4

Notes

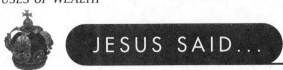

JESUS SAID...

Week 3, Day 5

THE REAL REASON FOR WEALTH

Scripture Verses

"The grass withers and the flowers fall, but the word of our God stands forever."

–Isaiah 40:8

"What good is it for a man to gain the whole world, and yet lose or forfeit his very self?"

–Luke 9:25

I n today's study, you'll look at three more reasons people accumulate money and conclude by studying *the one and only valid reason* God supplies wealth to Christians.

4.   **Self-esteem** — Many people, including Christians, use money in an attempt to buy esteem for themselves or their families. They want people to cater to them, to elevate them, and to yield to their way. They never share with anyone except to promote themselves. A Christian cannot accumulate for self-worth within God's plan. Esteem and importance will fade as quickly as the money does. See Isaiah 40:8 at left.

Have you ever acquired things to impress others? If so, tell about it here. *(Example: I bought a car that far exceeded my needs in order to brag about my large income. I felt this made me important. During that time, I was giving very little to God's work.)*

_____

_____

5.   **The love of money** — Those who genuinely love money for money's sake wouldn't part with it for anything — not even for esteem. Hoarding characterizes their lives. They may have accumulated thousands, tens of thousands, or even millions, but the loss of even a few dollars is traumatic. They become embittered, nervous, frustrated, and angry when others invade their financial domain. This is a form of idol worship, just as surely as worshiping pagan images of clay or metal.

Unfortunately, many Christians cling to every material possession they can. Trapped by the love of money, they would let their families do without rather than to part with their things. The love of money invites the discipline of God.

Read Luke 9:25 at left. Does this bring conviction to you? Have you ever pursued "gaining the whole world" while you forfeited yourself? If so, describe.

_____

_____

Week 3, Day 5

Scripture Verses

6. **Protection** — On the surface, accumulating money for protecting yourself sounds proper. However, Christians sometimes do this because they don't really trust God enough to believe He can supply their needs, so they begin to stash it away. Enough money never exists for people with this attitude. They may also obtain large amounts of life, casualty, disability, or liability insurance, or massive amounts of any assets. None of those is bad within itself; only through misuse do they corrupt. But anxiety over the future traps many Christians into over-protection, to the detriment of His kingdom work. Having stepped out of God's will, they no longer trust Him.

7. **A spiritual gift: God's true reason** — God supplies wealth to a Christian for only one reason: so that person will have enough to provide for others' needs. Because true wealth comes with the gift of giving, God promises His blessings on all who freely give and promises His curse on those who hoard, steal, covet, or idolize. At right, Paul defines the reason for having wealth as meeting the needs of the saints. The gift of giving is defined as the foundation for a life of selfless devotion to others.

"You will be made rich in every way so that you can be generous on every occasion, and through us your generosity will result in thanksgiving to God."
—2 Corinthians 9:11

The risks of being a wealthy Christian are enormous because of the temptations. You can step outside God's plan simply by attitude. See the verses in Proverbs at right. Becoming content without God in your abundance is a much more subtle sin than stealing. You simply slip outside of God's will and never realize it until calamity hits.

" . . . give me neither poverty nor riches, but give me only my daily bread. Otherwise, I may have too much and disown you and say, 'Who is the Lord?'"
—Proverbs 30:8-9a

If you are making money and not sharing it, you can be certain you are not within God's will. Watch for the symptoms that reveal God's principles are being violated: sacrifice of friends, health, family, and personal relationship with Jesus Christ to the pursuit of wealth. Attitudes characterized by bitterness, anxiety, frustration, or worry are also warnings. Remember that one day you will stand before God and give an account of what you have done with His resources.

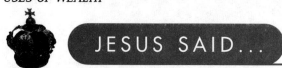

This Week

Scripture Verses

"Search me, O God, and know my heart; test me and know my anxious thoughts. See if there is any offensive way in me, and lead me in the way everlasting."
        –Psalm 139:23-24

THE REAL REASON FOR WEALTH *continued . . .*

Go to the Lord in prayer. Ask Him to search your heart in regard to what you read in the last paragraph and the passage at left. Prayerfully consider your answers to the following questions.

- Am I making money and not sharing it? If so, where does God want me to share?

- Are there any of the symptoms that show a violation of God's principles?

- How will I measure up when I stand before God and give an account of what I've done with His resources?

Week 3, Day 5

Notes

JESUS SAID...

ACT RESPONSIBLY, NOW

This Week

Scripture Verses

"But godliness actually is a means of great gain, when accompanied by contentment. For we have brought nothing into the world, so we cannot take anything out of it either."
–1 Timothy 6:6-7, NASB

One of the greatest gifts a person can leave to his or her family is a legacy of sound finances. In contrast, few things are sadder than observing a family attempt to sort through the financial disarray and confusion after the death of a loved one, compounded by the emotional stresses of the loss. There is great peace and contentment in making plans for all that we must surely leave behind. See the verses from 1 Timothy at left.

If you desire to minister to your loved ones after you die, one fact is certain: order and the clarity of your intentions won't occur accidentally. Rather, leaving a legacy of sound finances will occur because you took the time to plan that transition. Is your estate organized? Do you have a will?

If you have an inheritance to pass on to the next generation, good stewardship dictates that you use discernment in doing so. How much (what amount) is appropriate and healthy to pass on to loved ones? Should you leave assets to unbelieving children? Should you leave some children more than you do others? Can you structure the transfer of material wealth to minimize the tax liability? These are important questions, in light of the fact that researchers now estimate that between $41 and $136 trillion (that's with a *T*) of material assets may transfer hands in the next half century.[1] That sum could represent either a remarkable stride toward funding the Great Commission (if the Lord doesn't return first) or a colossal squandering of assets.

The question is not what the rest of Christendom is doing, but what *you* are doing to faithfully pass on your assets to the next generation. You may be in your twenties or thirties and say to yourself, "I don't have to worry about that now. I have a lot of living to do." Or you may think you don't have much in the way of assets, anyway. Well, you may and you may not! Today, most people have the ability to create a large estate. It may be land, business, homes, vehicles, other personal effects, or an insurance policy payable upon your death, but nevertheless, it is an estate. What then?

This week's study will help you identify the issues related to leaving a Christian legacy as well as key steps you can take now to ensure that your assets will continue serving Christ long after you have left this earth.

Week 4, Day 1

Scripture Verses

In truth, no generation of people has ever managed more material assets with less training to do so. In the time span of a single generation, an individual can go from near poverty to an estate of millions of dollars. Unfortunately, the succeeding generation can just as quickly lose it all. We seem to be a people of extremes, and inheritance is no exception. One part of society leaves enormous wealth to its generally untrained offspring.

You have already studied about the latter group as you've made your way through the *Jesus On Money* studies and contemplated good stewardship. It is sufficient to say that many Christians who spend all that they have without regard to their children are not good stewards. In fact, the legacy that many Christian parents leave today is one of debt.

If I had to identify the area of Christian finances that people least understand, it is inheritance. Not only do many people wreck their lives by hoarding, they also wreck the lives of their children and grandchildren with a too-abundant inheritance. In the parable of the Prodigal Son, Luke 15:11-14, you can see the result of giving large amounts of money to those who are unprepared for its use.

Read Luke 15:11-14 at right and answer these questions.

What is one advantage of the son having asked the father for his inheritance in the time frame in which he did?

_____

_____

What degree of training do you believe the young man had in the use of money?

_____

_____

What trouble came to the son as a result of his receiving the inheritance?

_____

_____

" . . . There was a man who had two sons. The younger one said to his father, 'Father, give me my share of the estate.' So he divided his property between them. Not long after that, the younger son got together all he had, set off for a distant country and there squandered his wealth in wild living. After he had spent everything, there was a severe famine in that whole country, and he began to be in need."
                    –Luke 15:11-14

69

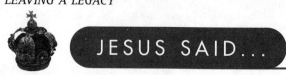

JESUS SAID...

ACT RESPONSIBLY, NOW *continued . . .*

This Week

Scripture Verses

"I know your deeds, your love and faith, your service and perseverance, and that you are now doing more than you did at first."

–Revelation 2:19

At least the father in this parable had enough sense to give his son the inheritance while the father was living. He then had the opportunity to provide the boy with counseling. Although he had the chance to counsel him, no evidence in the Bible suggests that the young man was properly trained in the use of money. As you see, the result of the inheritance was trouble for the recipient: wasted resources, straying into a wicked lifestyle, family disgrace.

I once counseled a man who had accumulated a sizeable estate. When I asked him what he planned to do with it all, he said, "I'll leave it to my children, I guess." I asked him why he didn't just give it to them right then, and he replied, "Why, they don't know how to handle money; they'd just lose it all." When asked if he thought they wouldn't lose it after he died, his response was, "Well, I'll be gone then, so who cares?" Well, God cares, because being a good steward doesn't stop with death. Read Revelation 2:19 at left.

Have you ever, or do you now, have the "I'll be gone, so who cares?" attitude about planning now for your financial legacy? Describe how you feel about leaving a legacy.

_____

_____

_____

Poor stewardship also can mean leaving a spouse who is unequipped to take over managing the finances. Unfortunately, that is most often the case. The results are anxiety, frustration, and dependence on unwise counselors. Generally, the wife is the surviving spouse. You would think that men would believe the statistics that show that seven out of eight men die before their wives do. Apparently they don't. Consequently, many women are forced into the role of estate manager with little or no knowledge in that area. To make matters worse, their husbands leave few guidelines for them to follow. In fact, in almost 70 percent of the cases, they don't even leave a valid will. Failure to make a will leaves the asset distribution up to the state.

Further, the average man leaves about 20 percent of the minimum assets necessary to provide for his family. That includes total life insurance of about $20,000, or about the same average as in 1963. Why is this? Does the

Week 4, Day 1

average American father truly not care about his family? I don't think so. I believe it really boils down to two flaws: ignorance and slothfulness — ignorance, because most people haven't been taught good stewardship, which includes inheritance; and slothfulness, because many people know what they should do but procrastinate until it's too late.

How do you feel when you think about discussing the type of inheritance you will provide? Check any of the following statements that apply.

❑ It's scary. I'm terrified to even think (much less talk) about dying.
❑ Superstitious. I'm afraid that if I discuss it, it might occur.
❑ I don't like to dwell on gloomy subjects. I'd rather just be carefree and enjoy each day.
❑ I'm in good health. My "time of need" is a long way off. Why waste my efforts now on this subject?
❑ Interested. I've never done much thinking in this area. I realize I need to be more aware.
❑ Relieved. I've already taken care of these matters responsibly.
❑ Other _____

Some Christians are superstitious without realizing it and avoid discussing death for fear that will cause it to occur. However, unless the Lord comes first, death will occur for each of us. Talking about death neither hastens nor delays it. It only makes things easier for those left behind. See the verse from Proverbs at right.

Ask God for help as you give thought to what steps you can take. Perhaps you need to ask Him to take away your fear of thinking about death. Perhaps you need to ask him for boldness to step outside your comfort zone or for objectivity and clarity as you plan. Trust that you can appeal to Him with "all kinds of prayers and requests," as Ephesians 6:18 says, even on this subject.

[1] David Cay Johnston, "A Larger Legacy May Await Generations X, Y, and Z," *The New York Times on the Web*, October 20, 1999, www.nytimes.com/99/10/20/news/financial/.

"A simple man believes anything, but a prudent man gives thought to his steps."
    –Proverbs 14:15

"And pray in the Spirit on all occasions with all kinds of prayers and requests. With this in mind, be alert and always keep on praying for all the saints."
    –Ephesians 6:18

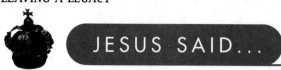

JESUS SAID...

Week 4, Day 2

This Week

Scripture Verses

"A good man leaves an inheritance for his children's children, but a sinner's wealth is stored up for the righteous."
  –Proverbs 13:22

"Command them to do good, to be rich in good deeds, and to be generous and willing to share. In this way they will lay up treasure for themselves as a firm foundation for the coming age, so that they may take hold of the life that is truly life."
  –1 Timothy 6:18-19

GUIDANCE FROM THE BIBLE

God leaves no life issue untouched in His Word. Fortunately that includes the area of inheritance. Even a brief survey of the Bible reveals that God provided for each generation through inheritance. In biblical times, the sons inherited their father's properties and thus provided for the rest of their family. See the verse at left.

What is not so obvious is that in most instances in Jewish tradition the sons received their inheritance while their fathers lived, as I mentioned earlier. This probably occurred when the oldest son reached his mid-thirties. Thus, a father was able to oversee his son's stewardship while he was still around to show him how to manage it. In the Prodigal Son parable, the father lived to see the younger son restored. I wonder what money management training most children would receive if their parents knew they would turn over all the estate to the children and depend on them for their support.

Obviously, the most important inheritance you can offer your children is a Christian influence that leads to salvation. Thankfully, most Christian parents don't leave that aspect of inheritance training until after death.

Have you worked on this part of inheritance training? If you have children (or, if you're single, if you have nieces or nephews or other children within your sphere of influence), are you certain that they have trusted Christ as Savior and have the assurance of eternal life? If you don't know this for sure about the young people in your life, what steps will you take to encourage them to trust Christ?

_____
_____
_____
_____

Equipping Your Spouse
Ensure that your spouse understands how to deal with money well. Although in many homes the husband is the primary money manager, in other instances the wife assumes this role, with the husband somewhat uninvolved in family finances. If your spouse has never actually managed the money, the training

Week 4, Day 2

starts with basic budgeting. Suggest that your spouse manage the home finances for at least the next year. One couple I know did this kind of inventive trade-off: the husband did the menu planning and grocery shopping for a year, and the wife paid the bills. Then, if one person is left, the surviving spouse can feel confident that he or she can manage the money, as well as the household.

I know a husband and wife who conduct a quarterly financial review of all their home finances. Although the husband is the primary financial person, at least once a quarter the couple sits down at the computer and reviews the family budgeting program, so the spouse knows about bill payment schedules and other matters.

If you are married, describe the arrangement you and your spouse use to keep each other informed about your home's money management. If you don't do this already, what would be necessary for you to begin such training?

_____

_____

_____

_____

Create a will(s) and/or trust(s)[1] — A will is the basic legal document for after-death asset distribution and is crucial for every living person. Without a will, the state in which you live will distribute your assets according to its laws of intestacy. (Intestacy means dying without a valid will.) Rarely, if ever, will this be according to your wishes. Husband and wife both need wills, with each understanding the other's will. First, pray about how you wish your estate to be distributed, including provision for the Lord's work. Then, write it out as clearly as possible and have a competent attorney write your plan into your will.

Some people think that as long as their properties are jointly owned they do not require wills, since the properties automatically revert to the survivor. However, depending on the size of your estate, significant estate taxes or

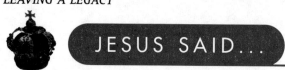

JESUS SAID...

GUIDANCE FROM THE BIBLE *continued . . .*

This Week

Scripture Verses

"A prudent man sees danger and takes refuge, but the simple keep going and suffer for it."
    –Proverbs 22:3

other difficulties can be avoided only through good estate planning. For example, if both of you were killed in an accident, and one of you died intestate, all jointly owned assets would be settled by the state, perhaps not to your liking. Invest the little time and money necessary to get a will for both you and your spouse. In most cases, a will costs less than $200 for a lawyer to write.

Some people think a letter suffices as a will. It's highly possible that it won't. Not only will the state decide how your assets are to be distributed, if you die intestate, the state will designate your children's guardians, if you are parents and your children are underage. The children typically go to the next living relative, regardless of whether or not this person shares your values. Accept your responsibility and have wills drawn up. See what Proverbs 22:3 says at left.

If you have underage children or other underage young people for whom you are responsible *(example: custody of grandchildren)*, **how have you dealt with custody issues? Whom have you designated as guardians for them, if no surviving parent were left?**

_____

_____

_____

I once counseled three Christian widows whose husbands died in the same airplane crash. All three had planned to have wills drawn, but only one had actually done so. Within three months, his estate was settled, the insurance proceeds securely invested, and the family resettled near the grandparents. The total legal bills amounted to less than $1,000.

The other two probate matters dragged on for years, with one of the women ultimately receiving a child's share of her husband's estate. One of the families contested its settlement, and it took nearly seven years and $25,000 to resolve what a $200 will could have settled in 30 days.

Both husbands who died without wills thought they didn't have estates large enough to worry about. The final insurance settlement from the crash was

Week 4, Day 2

more than $1 million apiece. It was more than enough to make a remote family member turn up and fight for a share.

Do you have a will? ❑ Yes ❑ No
Does your spouse (if you are married)? ❑ Yes ❑ No
Do you understand each other's will? ❑ Yes ❑ No

If you are not prepared in the area of wills, describe what steps you will take to act on this matter.

_____
_____
_____
_____

Some individuals or families need a *trust* in order to manage their assets to reduce estate costs and/or state taxes. Many varieties of trusts exist. Contrary to most opinions, their use is not limited to large estates. Almost any good bookstore or library will have several easy-to-read books on the use of wills and trusts. *Gift of a Lifetime: Planned Giving in Congregational Life*[2] by J. Gregory Pope is an excellent new resource which raises and answers many questions related to estate planning, including charitable giving and tax avoidance. Several large Christian ministries, such as Campus Crusade for Christ, Billy Graham Crusades, Christian Broadcasting Network, and agencies of various denominations, such as the International Mission Board of the Southern Baptist Convention, offer free estate-planning services for persons who plan to support their ministry. All of them provide good quality materials upon request.

If you name churches or other charitable organizations as beneficiaries, I suggest that you specify either a percentage or a dollar amount to be given. I also suggest you let the organization know beforehand. Many church institutions are surprised and ill-prepared for gifts they had no idea had been left to them. This money then would be removed from the value of your estate for estate tax purposes. You can even place your home into a trust under what is called a "life estate," in which you give up ownership but retain

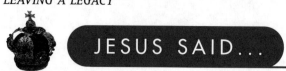

JESUS SAID...

Week 4, Day 2

GUIDANCE FROM THE BIBLE *continued* . . .

the right to live there during your lifetime. When you die, all assets in trust will go immediately to the charitable organizations according to the terms you decided on, and these assets will not be taxed. The portion going to the Lord's work will be protected from taxation. You'll read more about this in Day 5.

Because this involves highly specialized estate-planning law, I suggest you contact a good Christian attorney in your area to have this person deal with the entire estate plan for you.

[1] J. Gregory Pope, "The Christian Will: A Legacy of Faith and Love" (Nashville: LifeWay, 1999), 0-6330-0708-0 (Pamphlet)

[2] J. Gregory Pope, *Gift of a Lifetime: Planned Giving in Congregational Life* (Nashville: Broadman & Holman, 1999), 0-8054-1848-2

Week 4, Day 2

Notes

JESUS SAID...

Week 4, Day 3

DEVELOP A PLAN

Besides the legal instruments necessary to distribute and manage your estate, you also need a plan. For instance, at what age do you want to begin training your children? How much will you entrust to their management? Who will advise them? Obviously, each family's plan will be somewhat different, but the one common factor for Christians can be an understanding of God's principles for managing money. Again, if you don't have children in the home but have grandchildren or other children on whom you have an influence, these tips can apply to you.

Age — No best age exists to start teaching children good money management but the younger, the better. For very young children, start their training by helping them understand the value of money. Start this by associating money with work. Pay them small sums for tasks around the home; then help them decide whether to spend it or save it.[1] As they get older, begin to expand their training, including a good study of God's principles.

Practice — Nothing helps more to reinforce principles than problems. As your children approach the teen years, put them into real-life money situations. Let them open checking and savings accounts and do the monthly balancing. Allow them to manage their clothing budget.

Borrowing — The principle of borrowing can best be demonstrated by lending money to them at interest and requiring that they repay the loan — totally. Many young couples would have been better off if their parents had taught them about debt while they were living at home, rather than waiting for a creditor to do it.

Investing — Young people can clearly see the risk-reward system of our economy if you entrust to them a sum of money (small at first) to be invested. A teenager who has his or her money at risk suddenly sees how real the economy and money can become. I once helped each of our sons get involved in an area of investing to demonstrate how free enterprise really works. For one, it was a car to fix up and resell; for another, it was repairing a small rental house; for another, it was a small coin investment. The cost to me was relatively small; the *real* reward was helping to develop three free-market enthusiasts!

Week 4, Day 3

Giving — Teach your children to give to God's work out of their earnings, and you have made what I personally believe is the most essential step in molding them into good money managers. "Train a child in the way he should go, and when he is old he will not turn from it" (Proverbs 22:6).

Put stars by the previous suggestions that the Lord is leading you to try. Below, describe one experience you had in teaching one of these principles to another generation. Be prepared to share your experience with your group.

_____

_____

_____

Rarely will you find a generous giver who manages money poorly. God promises wisdom to those who trust Him; both managing and giving are evidences of that trust.

Large amounts of money given to children will often be squandered to their disservice, and large amounts of money stored up for children in trust can be used to buffer them from God's will. See the verse from Proverbs at right.

Reread that last paragraph and underline it. Give an example of how you may have seen this happen (or how you can envision it happening in someone's life). Too much money hoarded for children to inherit buffers them from God's will.

_____

_____

_____

"Folly is bound up in the heart of a child, but the rod of discipline will drive it far from him."
–Proverbs 22:15

You might have answered that children who think they can avoid work because they have a vast inheritance stored away for them might not be motivated to get proper education or learn a skill. It might prevent them from some of the life experience the work world teaches and from seeking to know God's purpose for them.

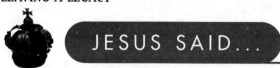

JESUS SAID...

Week 4, Day 3

This Week

Scripture Verses

"In him we have redemption through his blood, the forgiveness of sins, in accordance with the riches of God's grace that he lavished on us with all wisdom and understanding."
                –Ephesians 1:7-8

DEVELOP A PLAN *continued . . .*

Is that really your wish? Allow your children the joy of earning their own way. That doesn't mean to impoverish them. Provide for your family, but do not buffer them from God's will or life experiences with great hoards of money.

God's will regarding passing on money to one's children is partly expressed in Ecclesiastes 6:3, "A man may have a hundred children and live many years; yet no matter how long he lives, if he cannot enjoy his prosperity and does not receive proper burial, I say that a stillborn child is better off than he." This denotes the necessity of leaving the family *some* provision. This man didn't accumulate enough to even get a proper burial, let alone provide for his children. God said that as a godly person you leave your children's children an inheritance, but that inheritance is spiritual.

See the verses at left. Underline some things that are a part of that spiritual inheritance. Stop and thank God that He gave you this inheritance, which is far more important than any other.

[1] Wesley D. Center, "Kaitlyn and the Three Jars" (Nashville: LifeWay, 1998), 0-7673-3092-7 (Pamphlet)

Week 4, Day 3

Notes

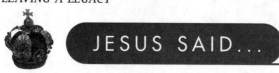

MORE ABOUT YOUR CHILDREN

This Week

Scripture Verses

"Now I am ready to visit you for the third time, and I will not be a burden to you, because what I want is not your possessions but you. After all, children should not have to save up for their parents, but parents for their children."

–2 Corinthians 12:14

A few more comments are important to note about giving an inheritance to your children. Again, understanding biblical principles behind inheritance is important. We know that the parent has a responsibility to store up for his or her children. See what Paul says in the verse at left. Even though Paul refers in this passage to spiritual values, I also believe he refers to finances, since that is a major theme of 2 Corinthians.

Each husband and wife are to decide how much to pass on as an inheritance, based on God's plan for their lives. Scripture leaves the choices to the parents. Parents must evaluate both the management abilities and the financial needs of their children to decide how to allocate the assets.

An inheritance is meant to be a "living gift," meaning that it's given before death, unless a parent suffers an untimely death. But, regardless of when your children receive their inheritance, I encourage you not to give it all at one time, and particularly not at an early age. Giving it to them in successive portions, perhaps beginning at age 25 through age 35 or 40, is best. That way the errors of youth can be overcome. As a parent, you will be able to provide godly counsel as your child makes use of his or her inheritance.

If you have already taken this step and have begun giving a portion of your money to your children, summarize below what you've done. Be prepared to share your experience with your group. If you've not yet taken this step, describe below what hesitation you might have and what would be necessary for you to begin this plan, when the time is appropriate.

_____

_____

_____

_____

_____

Should you distribute your assets to unsaved children? That is also an issue for each couple or individual to determine. I find no scriptural principle directing a believer to exclude an unsaved child from his or her rightful

Week 4, Day 4

Scripture Verses

portion of an inheritance, provided that the child isn't anti-Christian, such as being involved in a cult. What that portion is exactly is up to the individual/ couple and God. Because it's all God's property, be careful to distribute those assets according to God's wishes and desires rather than your own.

If your children are involved in a cult or perhaps a lifestyle that includes alcohol, other drugs, or homosexual practices, remember that the money you have belongs to God, not to you. You are only the steward of it. Use the Lord's money wisely. Would He want it to go to fund substances, circumstances, or precepts that lead people away from Him? In this situation, tell your child why you can't include him or her in your will. If necessary, put the funds in a trust, stating that your child can't have access to them as long as he or she is involved in the cult or in such harmful practices. Then select a person whom you trust to serve as trustee, and give him or her the power to determine the distribution. This might alienate your child, but take comfort in what Jesus says in the verse at right. Assure your children that you still love them and pray for them daily.

"Anyone who loves his father or mother more than me is not worthy of me; anyone who loves his son or daughter more than me is not worthy of me . . . ."
–Matthew 10:37

Scripture is clear: as long as your children are under your care, you have a responsibility to support them. However, if they are no longer dependent on you, the assets are yours to do with as you believe God leads. If you don't want to leave anything to your children, you don't have to.

I counsel you to pray about this, discuss it with your spouse if you are married, and be absolutely sure that you are following God's direction. Don't use your assets to get even with your children. Possibly, by leaving them something, you would have one last opportunity to share the message of salvation with them. As I mentioned earlier, another alternative is to leave something in trust that would be paid out later under very specific and controlled conditions.

There are many creative ways a parent can give to children. Establishing savings accounts, educational accounts for their children, IRAs, and many other giving avenues are more fully discussed in *Gift of a Lifetime: Planned Giving in Congregational Life* by J. Gregory Pope. (See page 76.)

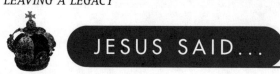

JESUS SAID...

This Week

MORE ABOUT YOUR CHILDREN *continued . . .*

Go back and underline any phrases or sentences that Jesus is speaking to you about; they may apply to decisions you've made already or circumstances with which you are struggling. Then pray about them. Consider asking your prayer partner to join you to intercede about these important matters. Summarize your thoughts and questions in a brief, written prayer. Come back to this page as you complete this study until God gives you clear direction.

_____

_____

_____

_____

_____

_____

_____

_____

Week 4, Day 4

Notes

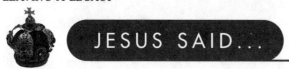

Week 4, Day 5

GIVE TO GOD'S WORK

In your Day-1 study, you read that being a good steward doesn't end with death. This week, you've seen that God expects you to make sound decisions now that impact how His money will continue to be used after you die. You've studied about using discernment in deciding whether your children have shown themselves to be responsible by using God's money (as given to them by you) wisely.

Now, spend a few more minutes looking at how God's work can be accomplished after you leave this life.

Many churches and church-related agencies offer special ways that you can set up funds to continue ministering long after you are deceased. These funds do not always require enormous sums, either. Some causes "pool" gifts from several estates in order to benefit one project. The government even encourages this sort of giving through the laws reducing the tax burden on the entire estate because of a charitable gift.

Before you consider which method to select, study about why you might want to do this.

Some people believe that because they have tithed their entire Christian lives, they have "paid their dues." Therefore, no further giving is necessary. That attitude misses the point. The tithe is the minimum. It is a standard by which you measure, but it is not the end of giving. Besides, most people do not tithe the increase that occurs with the value of their possessions — the increase that the government calls capital gains when these possessions are sold.

Consequently, many Christians desire to leave some of their estate to Christian causes as a reflection of how they have lived and as a testimony to their faith. Some do this because they consider the size of their estates and believe they might harm their children spiritually by leaving them too much money. Others who donate to Christian causes realize their successful offspring do not need the money. Still others want to leave their children a legacy of knowing that Mom and/or Dad left neither debts nor a large sum of money to be eaten up in taxes.

Week 4, Day 5

Assess your estate realistically. Don't put a high value on something you know is valueless. Likewise, don't overlook the appreciation that can occur sometimes almost quietly: perhaps an old stock purchase or some inherited land or mineral rights. Also, know how your estate stacks up against current tax laws. For years, the federal government taxed everything beyond $600,000 left in an estate to non-spouses and beyond $1.2 million left to a spouse. That cap is slowly rising today. Perhaps by the time you read this it will have risen several hundred thousand dollars. Many people are surprised to discover that when all their assets are analyzed, their estates (personal possessions, including expensive jewelry, home, savings plans, particularly 401(k)s and IRAs, pensions, stocks, and so forth) amount to much more than the current cap.

Have you determined the total value of your estate? ❏ **Yes** ❏ **No**
Have you determined what portion you desire to use for Christian purposes after your death? ❏ **Yes** ❏ **No**

Don't let tax planning be your only motive for giving to God's work. Some want to leave a large portion of their estates; others feel comfortable with only a token amount. These are decisions that only you can make — and in a timely fashion. The government wants as much as it can take when you are gone. A childless widow I know has an estate valued at more than $1 million. She has determined that she wants everything to go to her surviving nieces and nephews, whom she views as her children. Nevertheless, depending on when she dies and how much the estate increases between now and then, her heirs may have to pay $150,000 or more in estate taxes — money that otherwise could have gone to her church or favorite Christian organization, if she had planned differently.

If you decide to leave some part of your estate to the work of the Lord, the opportunities may seem boundless. Examine your own life. Have you focused your time on a certain aspect of ministry? Did you go overseas on volunteer missions trips? Did you concentrate your attention on inner-city ministries to the down-and-out? Were you most interested in seeing one particular segment of American culture or one particular group overseas come to know Jesus as Lord? Was ministering in your church's media library your

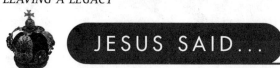

JESUS SAID...

Week 4, Day 5

This Week

Scripture Verses

"I will instruct you and teach you in the way which you should go; I will counsel you with My eye upon you. Do not be as the horse or as the mule which have no understanding, Whose trappings include bit and bridle to hold them in check, Otherwise they will not come near to you."

–Psalm 32:8-9, NASB

GIVE TO GOD'S WORK *continued . . .*

calling, or have you read about the need for drilling water wells in an arid, non-Christian country and wished you could help?

Underline any of the above that apply. If none do, describe here some areas of ministry that appeal to you or that represent your interests.

_____

_____

_____

_____

Have you prayed and sought God's direction on whether to leave any portion of your estate to the causes you mentioned above? ❑ Yes ❑ No If not, why not?

_____

_____

_____

The Scripture at left promises God's counsel as you seek direction. After you read these verses, write a short prayer, commiting to follow His counsel.

_____

_____

_____

_____

Once you determine to do this and know where you would like your surplus to go, the next question is just as important: How? Some want to set up trusts in their lifetime to begin to see the benefits as well as to make sure everything is in proper order.

I urge you to discuss this with your attorney first. I presume that you have chosen an attorney who is a Christian and whose life reflects dedication to the Lord. Don't be fooled by religious talk or by some quick answer. Ask about a prospective attorney's legal training as well as his or her relationship to the Lord and commitment to the church. You may want to ask Christian friends

Week 4, Day 5

Scripture Verses

for recommendations. A good attorney will not try to steer you toward his or her favorite project but will listen for your wishes.

Write the initials of your attorney or of a Christian attorney who comes to mind. _____

As you read the verse at right, pray for this potential counselor and ask God to reveal His purposes.

"Many are the plans in a man's heart, but it is the Lord's purpose that prevails."
                    –Proverbs 19:21

Other excellent sources of information are your pastor and the development officers at your favorite ministry agency or institution. Again, check out the entity's reputation before you proceed. No institution worthy of your contribution needs to fear your inquiries or scrutiny. Most welcome such inquiries.

You may want to inquire about how well-endowed a particular ministry is and determine how it spends its resources. I once knew of a church that had a beautiful building, well-educated staff, and huge endowment, but its ministry languished and its pews were nearly empty on Sunday mornings. Putting more funds into that church's endowment did not appear to be the best use of someone's surplus. It may have actually hindered the church's growth.

The array of ways you can give your surplus to the Lord's causes is also diverse. Some people merely donate the money outright. Tax laws are complicated, but the right approach can actually multiply the dollars given while saving you taxes. Giving an asset that has appreciated in value can help you avoid capital gains taxes and sometimes reap an actual tax write-off. Charities are allowed to provide annuities, gift annuities, and a host of other products. Please discuss these with your advisor.

Did you know, for example, that you could give away money, say $10,000 through a "gift annuity," and actually receive a tax deduction while you continue to receive interest on the money (often at a higher rate than you could receive at a bank or other savings institution)? These gift annuities can even be arranged to cover your lifetime and perhaps that of a spouse, child, or grandchild. This type of annuity is particularly useful if you want to provide

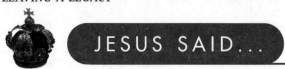

GIVE TO GOD'S WORK *continued . . .*

support after you die for someone who is mentally or emotionally handicapped.

Consider whether or not you want these gifts to draw attention to yourself or a loved one. You can make some gifts so that a building or particular room in a church, for example, is named for you or for someone you choose. Some people give money to a college and thus have their name engraved on a brick walkway. You may want to honor your mother, father, deceased spouse, or child. Some gifts are shrouded in anonymity. For some, the recognition is serene and dignified.

While some of these matters seem to be filled with tedious details, remember that God cares about the details. Pray about how He wants you to partner with Him so that your legacy becomes a living one that continues into eternity.

Week 4, Day 5

Notes

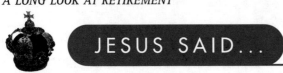

JESUS SAID...

This Week

Scripture Verses

"By wisdom a house is built, and through understanding it is established; through knowledge its rooms are filled with rare and beautiful treasures."
　　　　–Proverbs 24:3-4

" . . . but at the age of fifty, they must retire from their regular service and work no longer."
　　　　–Numbers 8:25

DEBUNKING THE RETIREMENT MYTH

The subject of retirement is something that confuses many Christians. Many people have developed something akin to a mania about retirement savings and the so-called necessity for storing up large amounts of assets. Many people think they will retire and spend much more than they did during working years. This is rarely true. Once you set a pattern for living, it will not change substantially after retirement, except in many cases to go down. See the verses from Proverbs 24 at left. If you have learned to adjust your standard of living during your income years, then retirement will be a comfortable adjustment for you. The Christian who hoards money to be used for retirement is being deceived.

List a couple of ways you believe some lifestyle adjustments you have made during this study will help you when your income is less than it is today. (Example: Our family has curbed the pattern of eating out excessively. Learning to avoid automatically going out for dinner will help me for the rest of my life.) **If you are retired already, describe some ways the suggestions and practices in *Jesus On Money* are helping you live within your retirement income.**

_____
_____
_____
_____
_____
_____

Where does a retirement (and a retirement-savings) program fit into God's plan? Since the Bible is your guide for day-to-day living, look at what you're doing, and planning, in comparison to that guide.

Actually, retirement, as you know it today, is found in only one place in God's Word. Numbers 8:25 at left refers to the retirement of the Levites from the tent of meeting. The Levites were directed not to own land or to accumulate riches but to receive their living from the tithes and offerings of God's people. As a reward for their service and obedience, they retired at age 50.

Week 5, Day 1

Scripture Verses

"For six years sow your fields, and for six years prune your vineyards and gather their crops. But in the seventh year the land is to have a sabbath of rest, a sabbath to the Lord. Do not sow your fields or prune your vineyards."
                    –Leviticus 25:3-4

Other than that single event, the people were not directed to retire. That does not mean they could not retire but that it was not normal. The normal system of retirement that you see throughout God's Word takes the form of a sabbatical. The first sabbatical given was a day of rest each week called the Sabbath. Additionally, the Jew was required to let his land lay idle every seventh year. See Leviticus 25:3-4 in the margin.

Wouldn't it be great to take retirement through sabbaticals? That would mean you would work six years and take the seventh off. You might use that year for continued education, missions work, new technology training, or simply to enjoy your family while you are still young.

Think imaginatively for a moment. If that principle (six years on, one year off) were possible for you, what would you do with your seventh year? What is something you'd love to do, if time and money permitted? Perhaps it's one of the ideas mentioned in the previous paragraph or something else you have in mind.

_____

_____

_____

_____

_____

_____

If you take seriously the concepts in *Jesus On Money*, particularly the ones in this chapter, as they build on what you've already learned, the type of lifestyle or life plan that you just described won't be as far-fetched as it seems. You can truly use your skills and the provision God has made for you to have a period of rest in which you seek to honor God in ways appropriate to your situation.

Ask God to give you an open heart and mind as you ponder some of this week's ideas, which may stretch your thinking considerably.

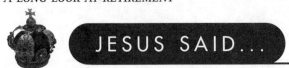

JESUS SAID...

Week 5, Day 2

A NEW CONCEPT OF RETIREMENT

Not all retirement is wrong anymore than all borrowing is wrong. It is a matter of degree. The problem is that people seem to do everything to excess today. In some professions, such as athletics, age is a critical factor, and retirement is inevitable. In other professions, everyday stress burns a person out.

But other instances exist in which retirement is encouraged in order to attract workers to retire. You often see this in government-related jobs, for example.

Retirement provides at least some benefits to society: (1) it makes room for younger, more aggressive people to be able to progress; (2) the shift to a lesser income at retirement necessitates a moderated lifestyle; and (3) the goal of retirement creates savings that can be used to help build and create jobs for others.

The biggest liability associated with retirement today is the mass notion that retirement is mandatory. The truth is that the majority of those over 65 cannot afford to retire, and we cannot afford for them to retire, because they will become wards of the state due to their lack of preparedness.

But since the idea of retirement has been sold to Americans during the last 40 years, we now accept it as normal. Sometimes people say they are "put out to pasture" at age 65, as though they no longer have something to contribute. The idea is that retirement is the period of time in your latter years when you can simply stop work and start enjoying life. This idea is not normal, either biblically or historically. Certainly some people exist who can retire, and there are a few who should, but most people (particularly Christians) have many options besides traditional retirement.

Retirement for Christians ideally means freeing time to devote to serving others more fully without the necessity of getting paid for it. If Christian retirees have this motivation in mind while they look forward to retirement, then the Lord will really find them doing His work when He returns.

A second liability is the fact that people take money that is needed for God's work and divert it into retirement plans. Many of those funds never will be

Week 5, Day 2

used because they far exceed the reasonable amount the retiree will need. Other funds won't be used because they will be lost or dissipated by inflation long before retirement. For retirement, only allocate funds that are left after giving what God has directed and after meeting family needs.

How much are you regularly saving for retirement?

_____

Based on what you have studied here already, is it possible that some of this saving is excessive and could be redirected to God's work? Describe your thoughts as you read this.

_____
_____
_____
_____

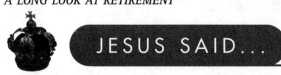

JESUS SAID...

STAYING USEFUL

Scripture Verses

"Don't let anyone look down on you because you are young, but set an example for the believers in speech, in life, in love, in faith and in purity."
–1 Timothy 4:12

"And he told them this parable: 'The ground of a certain rich man produced a good crop. He thought to himself, "What shall I do? I have no place to store my crops." 'Then he said, "This is what I'll do. I will tear down my barns and build bigger ones, and there I will store all my grain and

continued in right margin . . .

You may be conditioned to believe that people lose their usefulness when they are 60 or 65 years old. But today you can observe people everywhere who are healthy, vital, and truly in their prime of life during those years. Many of the apostles did their greatest work after the time you might consider them to be old men.

Name some of those useful older men and women of the Bible that come to mind.

_____

_____

You might have mentioned some like Abraham, Moses, Naomi, or Peter. The Bible says that Job recovered his fortune when he was in his older years.

Interestingly, when Paul admonished Timothy not to let anybody mock him because of his youth (1 Timothy 4:12 in the margin), Timothy was older than 40 at the time. So, at what point should you retire? If you have a good, full life and enjoy what you do, you will be useful throughout your entire life, not just in the early years. Nothing is wrong with saving in moderation for retirement; but something is wrong with storing unnecessarily, believing that is the only way to provide for later years.

The other end of the range of God's will can be found in Luke 12:16-20 (beginning at left.) See if you can detect God's attitude through the parable that Jesus used to instruct His followers.

Did God condemn the man for his wealth? ❑ Yes ❑ No
What caused the man's downfall?

_____

_____

_____

The man's problem, as God saw it, wasn't his wealth. It was his attitude about hoarding when his income increased. Knowing he didn't have enough room in his barns, he decided to build larger barns to store his crops and then

Week 5, Day 3

Scripture Verses

have contentment without God. Rather than seeking God's plan for the surplus, he decided to store it away.

Nothing is wrong with retirement planning. But something is wrong with living for retirement. Nothing is wrong with saving either, except when the motive is protection against the world.

Reassess your attitudes. Are you really worried that if you don't store now you will have to do without later? Do you believe that God is capable of supplying in your old age, or is your faith a myth?

Answer the questions just posed. In light of what you just read, would Jesus say you are saving or hoarding for retirement?

_____

_____

_____

_____

my goods. And I'll say to myself, 'You have plenty of good things laid up for many years. Take life easy; eat, drink and be merry.'" 'But God said to him, "You fool! This very night your life will be demanded from you. Then who will get what you have prepared for yourself?"'
–Luke 12:16-20

We seem to be a society of extremes. We borrow, spend, and work excessively during our early years and then want to quit altogether. For the vast majority of people, retirement is literally an impossible dream. They spend everything they make on a current basis and will actually save very little toward retirement. Even worse, a majority of 65-year-olds will still owe on their homes for 10 years or more. They are still in debt at retirement age and find it impossible to reduce their income needs substantially. For them, retirement will mean near poverty and dependency on the government. We see them on the rolls of welfare and Social Security. They require the help of their own children, who are unable or unwilling to help because they are strapped financially by indulgent lifestyles. It is difficult to imagine that these older adults are following God's direction.

For that group, their imbalance reflects a total lack of planning for the future. Christians can be wise enough to realize that, as they get older, their ability to maintain their income declines. Savings laid aside and invested wisely at an

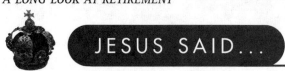

STAYING USEFUL *continued . . .*

early age can be used to supplement income needed at an older age, when they may still be able to work but for fewer hours or at less physically demanding jobs.

Have you considered doing this, or do you know anyone who has — continued to earn income in retirement years but at a scaled-back wage in a less physical job? If so, describe.

_____

_____

_____

_____

On the other side are Christians who have planned too well for retirement. They have enough stored away for at least three lifetimes already but continue to store even more. They have diverted funds that could be used to feed starving people and to change lives for eternity into a retirement account simply because it is a good tax shelter.

If we could convince American Christians to stop contributing to their retirement accounts for five years and to put every dime of that into missions, we would accomplish the Great Commission! If you don't decide "How much is enough?" you'll never truly be the steward God wants you to be.

What's your reaction to the statement I just made? Stop right now and pray; ask God if this is a challenge He wants you to take so that you can truly be on a mission with Him.

Week 5, Day 3

Notes

JESUS SAID...

HOW MUCH IS ENOUGH?

This Week

Scripture Verses

"For through me your days will be many, and years will be added to your life."

–Proverbs 9:11

Each Christian can realistically face some planning questions. If you've already retired, answer the questions below as they relate to your experience.

1. **Why should I retire?** You may be forced to retire because of your chosen vocation, such as that of an airline pilot or a professional athlete. Company policy may require you to retire at a certain age. But the decision may also be totally under your control; you may have the option of not retiring. See Proverbs 9:11 in the margin.

Have you considered retiring at an age later than 65, if your health and other life circumstances permit? ❑ Yes ❑ No   If yes, describe the plans you are considering.

_____

_____

_____

2. **What will I do?** Start now to get a clear picture of your life, post-work. How will you spend your time, and how will you keep involved with God's work?

_____

_____

_____

"Gray hair is a crown of splendor; it is attained by a righteous life."

–Proverbs 16:31

Without a doubt, our society isolates the elderly from the young. In doing so, we subvert God's plan for sharing learned wisdom. Make your plans to include involvement with younger families who need the benefit of your acquired wisdom. See Proverbs 16:31 at left.

Some ideas that come to mind for doing this:

_____

_____

(Example: I could teach a Sunday School class of young married couples, volunteer to tutor children in the neighborhood elementary school, mentor a

Week 5, Day 4

younger couple in marriage skills, take a group of young marrieds on a missions trip, volunteer child care to help some young parents in my neighborhood.)

3. **What if my retirement plans fail?** I am grieved to see so many of God's people depending on an economic system that is so clearly operating outside of God's wisdom. It no longer seems to be a question of what you will do *if* the economy fails, but what you will do *when* it does. Many Christians are tied up in intangible assets, such as stocks, which could be gone in a financial crisis. Perhaps the best retirement plan of all is a service skill that others need.

What skill do you have that you could use to provide for others? *(Example: repairing cars or appliances, cutting hair, computer skills, sewing, landscaping and yard care)*

_____

_____

4. **What if I can't retire?** Many Christians must simply give up the American concept of retirement and adjust their plans to include making a living for the rest of their lives. Therefore, if you fit into this category, plan your career by stages. The first stage would be to work until a given age (say, 50 to 55), with the goal of being totally debt free, including paying off your mortgage. Once your children are grown, seek retraining in a skill area that requires less physical strength — programming, accounting, art, or woodworking. These skills can successfully carry you through your lifetime.

In *Jesus On Money: Making Mid-Course Corrections*, **you studied about career transitions and the accompanying emotional traumas that sometimes occur when you suddenly shift gears. Below jot down some ways you think a graduated type of retirement, as described above, might be less difficult emotionally.**

_____

_____

_____

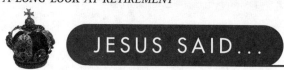

JESUS SAID...

Week 5, Day 4

HOW MUCH IS ENOUGH? *continued . . .*

Scripture Verses

"By wisdom a house is built, and through understanding it is established; through knowledge its rooms are filled with rare and beautiful treasures."
    –Proverbs 24:3-4

If you plan to transition as the previous plan outlines, you will never experience the stark break from workplace to home that a focus on job transition often describes. It won't be a matter of plunging yourself into work full steam ahead one day and then sitting at home in a rocking chair the next. You may not experience the same degree of adjustment difficulty as someone who goes "cold turkey," because you may still keep some of your former work contacts or responsibilities while you phase into new ones.

Clearly, any plan such as this requires consideration of both the husband's and wife's situations. For example, if the husband is the primary wage earner, then enough life insurance must be maintained to adequately provide for the wife. See Proverbs 24:3-4 in the margin.

Begin to honestly assess right now how much you will really need in your retirement years. Remember the distinction between wants and desires versus needs. How many clothes will be necessary, realistically? How much will be needed for food? What other needs will you have, such as insurance or housing? Consider that you may be able to cut back to one car, use less gasoline, downsize in housing, and make other scaled-down adjustments that will impact your overall budget and free other funds.

If you are already retired, describe the current situation and ask yourself if your want list could be reduced to free up other funds.

Clothing _____

Housing _____

Gasoline _____

Automobile _____

Travel _____

Insurance _____

Entertainment _____

Other _____

Week 5, Day 4

Notes

Reassess your needs for retirement. Perhaps you can take a portion of what you don't consider necessary and give it to the Lord's ministry today.

Thank God for how He has provided for you materially so far. Whether retirement is within a few years, has already occurred, or is decades away, ask Him to give you a realistic picture of wants versus needs in a scaled-down, retirement setting.

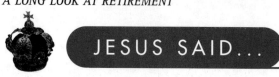

JESUS SAID...

Week 5, Day 5

PEOPLE GOD USES

I would like to share with you several case studies of real people who have refused to rust out in their retirement years. I've changed their names. They have continued serving God and their fellow human beings long after many people would have relaxed into more comfortable lifestyles.

Jack Camden worked as an analyst for a Fortune 500 company, and his wife June was a part-time instructor at a community college. They lived in a 3,500-square-foot house that overlooked a golf course. Their six grandchildren lived within a five-mile radius. Few people could have asked for a more ideal situation when they retired. But Jack and June didn't think God had blessed them during their younger years to merely spend their retirement days on the golf course. They sold their home and possessions and lived off the proceeds as they volunteered for an extended period of missions service overseas — Jack in the business area and June teaching English to nationals in the country where they served.

John Holmes had a successful career as an engineer. His wife of many years died just as he reached 65 and ended his official work career. Many of John's friends tried to persuade him to travel with them on cruises or on vacation trips to exotic places to help cheer him in his time of loss, but he declined. John believed the Lord hadn't gifted him with engineering skills to let them lie dormant. He and a relative began a project to help design water systems for communities that could not afford high-priced engineering help. He worked for only a fraction of the salary he earned as a professional but felt gratified that he was able to serve others.

Timothy and Ruth Malone spent 30 years as missionaries in Asia, serving much of that time in war-ravaged countries — some of the world's most difficult spots in which to minister. They came home to a much deserved period of rest, in the loving company of family members. Yet, within six months of their retirement, the Malones were back on the missions field, using their wisdom and experience to encourage new missionaries and living off the support their missions agency provided. When asked why she would uproot so quickly, Ruth replied, "I'd never turn down an opportunity to go back to people who need me." Her devotion to God's kingdom work didn't stop when she reached a certain age or stage in life.

Week 5, Day 5

A. W. Hill was a retired postal service worker in his senior years when God called him to preach. Until his late 90s, A. W. made daily visits to a nearby nursing home, where he read the Bible and brought cheer to the older adults, many of whom were 10 to 20 years younger than himself. He performed his last wedding and funeral when he was 98 years old, the last year before he died.

Go back to these four case studies. Underline any phrases or sentences that could also describe you and your outlook toward retirement. Put a star by anything you read that particularly inspires you.

Your retirement years could truly be your banner years, when you accomplish more but actually do less and without all the stress the early years of work have produced.

How might you begin now to plan for such a finale? Considering the vignettes you just read, what are some creative ways you can see yourself living and serving?

The first step I would take now would be to _____
_____
_____

One way I still need to bring my finances in order to prepare for retirement is
_____
_____
_____

Someone I could consult for advice about an adjusted approach to retirement is _____
_____

If you are married, close by praying knee-to-knee with your spouse. If you are single, ask a close friend or family member to pray with you regarding the matters you have studied here. Ask God to give you the faith to let Him, and not a bank account, take care of you in retirement.

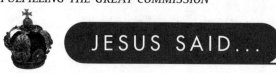

JESUS SAID...

THE CRY OF GOD'S HEART

This Week

Day 1: The Cry of God's Heart
Day 2: How to Get Started
Day 3: Taking a Major Step
Day 4: Ignite the Fire at Home
Day 5: Send the Light

Scripture Verses

" . . . *who wants all men to be saved and to come to a knowledge of the truth.*"

–1 Timothy 2:4

" . . . *(The Lord is) not wanting anyone to perish, but everyone to come to repentance.*"

–2 Peter 3:9b

" . . . *From everyone who has been given much, much will be demanded; and from the one who has been entrusted with much, much more will be asked.*"

–Luke 12:48b

The goal of financial freedom is remarkably bigger than merely becoming debt-free or consistently balancing your checkbook. The Bible does not teach prosperity for prosperity's sake. The goal of becoming financially free is not to enable you to spend unending days involved in leisure activities in exotic places. God desires for His people to be financially free for a specific purpose.

Read 1 Timothy 2:4 at left. What does this verse describe as God's heartthrob?

_____

_____

After you read this verse, you can imagine why God's heart breaks when you mismanage your resources. When you do not attain financial freedom, this hinders the sharing of the gospel. Ultimately, people die without ever achieving the thing for which God's heart beats: that people will hear of His saving grace in Jesus Christ. Read 2 Peter 3:9b at left.

The great passion of God — saving souls — can be your passion as well! Later in this week's study, you'll examine ways that, throughout various corners of the world, people are coming in huge numbers to faith in Jesus. People in areas such as Southeast Asia, South America, and Africa are experiencing great revivals, much like the revivals in the early history of the United States. You may want to consider moving your membership to a small, struggling church in your area. The infusion of your family's time, talents, and financial resources could make all the difference to that church and the people it serves.

Read what Jesus had to say in Luke 12:48b in the margin. Think how this verse applies to you. What have you been given?

_____

_____

_____

_____

_____

Week 6, Day 1

Scripture Verses

What is required of you?

_____
_____
_____
_____

No matter what you, or your church, has done already in the missions area, you can't be satisfied or, worse, compare your accomplishments to what other individuals or churches are doing around the world. Your call to fulfill the Great Commission must be based on nothing less than determining how God wants to use you in reaching the many people who have yet to hear the gospel. And remember, many of them are right in your own backyard.

Repeatedly the Bible teaches that God desires to reveal his great love for the world through His people.

Read the two Old Testament passages at right. Answer the following questions.

In Psalm 51:12-13, in the margin, what does King David say he will do if God grants forgiveness and restores fellowship following his adulterous episode with Bathsheba?

_____
_____
_____
_____

Why does the psalmist in Psalm 67:1-2 ask for God's blessings?

_____
_____
_____
_____

"Restore to me the joy of your salvation and grant me a willing spirit, to sustain me. Then I will teach transgressors your ways, and sinners will turn back to you."
      –Psalm 51:12-13

"May God be gracious to us and bless us and make his face shine upon us, that your ways may be known on earth, your salvation among all nations."
      –Psalm 67:1-2

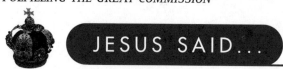

JESUS SAID...

Week 6, Day 1

This Week

Scripture Verses

"I will rescue you from your own people and from the Gentiles. I am sending you to them to open their eyes and turn them from darkness to light, and from the power of Satan to God, so that they may receive forgiveness of sins and a place among those who are sanctified by faith in me."

–Acts 26:17-18

"But you are a chosen people, a royal priest-hood, a holy nation, a people belonging to God, that you may declare the praises of him who called you out of darkness into his wonderful light."

–1 Peter 2:9

THE CRY OF GOD'S HEART *continued . . .*

This truth is also conveyed throughout the New Testament. Answer these questions, based on what you read at left.

In Acts 26:17-18, why does Paul say God saved him?

_____

_____

_____

In 1 Peter 2:9 at left, why does the apostle Peter declare that we have been saved?

_____

_____

_____

In all these instances, the writers indicate that God blesses so that you can make Him known. I can think of no greater motive for you to passionately pursue faithful stewardship in all matters other than what the Bible succinctly teaches: God loves the world and has given His Son so that souls will be saved for eternity!

Have you already seen some ways that getting your finances in good order, as you have done during your *Jesus On Money* study, has enabled you to be a missions-minded Christian in a more direct manner than ever before? If so, describe. *(Example: Because I reduced my budget and created a surplus, I was able to send money to a seminary in Romania that was attempting to rebuild its theological library.)*

_____

_____

_____

_____

_____

In prayer, thank Him for the benefit you just described. Ask God if He has a fresh work for you.

Week 6, Day 1

Notes

JESUS SAID...

This Week

Scripture Verses

"Like newborn babies, crave pure spiritual milk, so that by it you may grow up in your salvation, now that you have tasted that the Lord is good."

–1 Peter 2:2-3

HOW TO GET STARTED

"Okay," you reply. "I'm convinced. God expects me to be part of His kingdom mission. He's prospered me for a purpose. I'm motivated. But where and how can I start to do this?"

I'm not advocating that every Christian become a full-time career missionary, drawing a salary and support from such agencies as the International Mission Board, Wycliffe Bible Translators, or Youth with a Mission. Nor am I advocating that every evangelical Christian in America pack up and move overseas. Today, given modern transportation and communication systems, that is not always necessary.

To win the entire lost world to Jesus Christ, every Christian needs to take seriously the commitment to become a part of what God is doing all over the world and to contribute with talents and abilities that God has provided each individual. Because you have truly "tasted that the Lord is good" (1 Peter 2:3), you want others to know this too.

Some people may develop a prayer ministry: going to God regularly, interceding on behalf of a particular people group or a particular team of Christians working with that group.

Perhaps you've already begun this ministry. Check below any experiences you've had in praying for lost people.

❑ I participate regularly in my church's prayer ministry and pray for the lost of the world.

❑ I read the list of missionaries in my Sunday School quarterly and pray that God will strengthen them to reach others.

❑ I regularly call the prayer line of my denomination's missions agency and learn current prayer needs of missionaries around the world.

❑ My Bible study class has adopted people to pray for, and I intercede for these needs.

❑ My Bible study class has adopted a missionary to write, email, and pray for. I regularly intercede for these needs.

Week 6, Day 2

❑ I have participated in a prayer walk in my community that concentrated on a specific part of town, such as a university campus, an inner-city housing project, or a prison. During the prayer walk I prayed for lost people in that specific location.

❑ I have participated in a prayer walk in an overseas country, traveling there to pray on-site for specific needs.

❑ I'm praying about whether I should go on an overseas prayer walk.

❑ Even if I can't go personally, I'd like to contribute money for someone who would be blessed by going on an overseas prayer walk.

❑ Other (Describe here.) _____
_____
_____

Involvement can be as simple as this story tells. A Christian neighbor I know volunteers to provide child care for the three small children of a young mother so that the mother can pray regularly with and disciple a new believer from Japan. The Christian neighbor is "holding the coat" of the young prayer warrior so she can have direct involvement; that makes the neighbor a missions-minded Christian as well.

If you are not pressured with financial demands, and if your life is not consumed with surviving financially, you'll have more time to pray. And you'll be less stressed and more able to be in touch with the way the Holy Spirit stirs your heart for the needs of the lost world.

Others may develop a plan to save for volunteer missions trips, so that they or others might go. Today, incredible ways exist for Christians living in the United States to be able to minister for a few weeks over and over again, overseas. People who once thought themselves ineligible to become missionaries are finding remarkably creative avenues to reach out to lost people throughout the world. We know of more than 25,000 Southern Baptists who serve each year as volunteers, yet denominational officials believe that a number at least twice that size actually goes overseas each year to minister in creative and special ways.

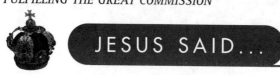

JESUS SAID...

Week 6, Day 2

This Week

Day 1: The Cry of God's Heart
Day 2: How to Get Started
Day 3: Taking a Major Step
Day 4: Ignite the Fire at Home
Day 5: Send the Light

HOW TO GET STARTED *continued . . .*

People once thought they were exempt from missions service because they were not preachers or evangelists. Today, every skill is needed. I know of a church that at one point thought it might have to cancel its volunteer trip to help rebuild homes in hurricane-ravaged Honduras because a Christian bricklayer needed for the construction team could not be found! Not only did the church find a brick mason, but as a result of going the man came to know Christ as his personal Savior.

One woman once told her denominational agency, "I have nothing to offer on a volunteer trip. I've been a homemaker, rearing my four children. I have no particular skill." But once persuaded to go, that homemaker played an amazing role. Impatient children, who waited with their parents in long lines to receive medicine in a Latin American medical clinic, were drawn to this woman as she sat nearby, animatedly reading stories from a picture book. Although she read in English, not in their native tongue, the children obviously sensed her caring, maternal spirit. What a ministry to the parents who stood in line!

Ten-year-old Holly accompanied her mother and others from their church on a missions trip to Honduras. She amazed all the volunteers and on-scene missionaries with her bold witness. Holly showed such love and concern for the children she visited in the hospital that the children's parents gladly listened as she shared her faith. She continues to be a winsome witness in her own neighborhood. Through her invitation, the mother of one of her friends visited Holly's church and heard the gospel. In only a few weeks, the woman gave her heart to Christ.

Have you ever served on a volunteer missions trip? ❏ **Yes** ❏ **No**
If not, have you ever considered doing so? ❏ **Yes** ❏ **No**
Is there a particular country or type of service to which you think God might be drawing you to volunteer? If so, list it here.

_____

_____

_____

_____

Week 6, Day 2

Again, such thoughts would seem totally out of the realm of possibility if you were mired in debt. Financial freedom enables you to think creatively and to be available when God calls.

Would you rather have your life count for something, or would you prefer to spend your leisure involved solely in the pursuit of self-serving interests? When your days on this earth are waning and you contemplate finding yourself face to face with your Maker — the One who gave you all your time, energy, and possessions — which choice do you think will be the most gratifying to you? See what Isaiah 40:8 at right says about choosing with eternity in mind.

List some ways that you can be involved now in missions outreach.

_____

_____

_____

_____

_____

_____

_____

As you close your day's work in prayer, give this choice some thought.

Scripture Verses

"The grass withers and the flowers fall, but the word of our God stands forever."
      –Isaiah 40:8

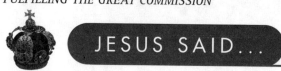

JESUS SAID...

Week 6, Day 3

TAKING A MAJOR STEP

Perhaps, either as you are completing your Book 3 study or at some time in the past, your heart has been stirred toward some permanent type of missions service. At one time, you may have decided to explore serving in the United States or overseas but have never acted on it. The need to complete your education, support a family, or deal with health concerns may have interfered at some point in your history. Possibly you now think, "I feel called to missions but can't devote my whole life to it." You may be responsible for the care of elderly parents or have some kind of health challenge or other life circumstance that would keep you from taking such a major, permanent step as career missions, but you still feel God tugging.

Where do you fit in this description? Answer the following questions.

In the past, have you ever felt God calling you to some type of missions service? ❑ **Yes** ❑ **No**

Did you ever make this decision public? Did you tell your church about it, talk with a pastor, contact a missions agency, or send off for material? If so, describe what you did.

_____

_____

_____

_____

What has happened since, as a result of this calling?

_____

_____

_____

_____

Since that time, have you ever wished you could do something to pursue that original decision but weren't sure how to proceed? ❑ **Yes** ❑ **No**

No longer must individuals feel, "Well, I once felt led to be a missionary, but I missed the opportunity in my younger years, so I guess it wasn't meant to be."

Week 6, Day 3

Scripture Verses

For people who feel the Lord calling them to become involved more than merely taking a few weeks of vacation and participating on a volunteer trip, some agencies provide short-term service stints. Individuals and couples can go overseas for periods of from four months to two years or sometimes longer.

This type of service period is ideal for people who may have taken early retirement. Perhaps their company offered it as an attractive package. They now have an abundance of time and are looking for ways to continue to use their talents and vitality. A short-term missions stint would allow them to experience life on a missions field firsthand and to see what God is doing overseas without having to make a lifetime commitment.

In these assignments, no special skills are required, but appointees capitalize on the talents God has given them and that they may have already used for years in their workplace or in their church service.

Someone might serve overseas as a treasurer for a missions team, an English-language teacher, a business manager, a teacher for the children of missionaries, a pharmacist for a medical clinic, a quilter or sewing instructor in a neighborhood setting, or in countless other needed roles.

It is not necessary to leave the United States in order to serve. God is equally concerned about your next-door neighbor or the folks living across the river from you who may not yet know Him as personal Lord and Savior. In missions agencies right here in North America, short-term personnel are assigned to sites such as campgrounds and resorts, on campuses in student ministry programs, in food kitchens serving the homeless, in low-income housing sites, in literacy work, and in community centers in disadvantaged parts of town, and other places.

Read the verses at right. What type of skills do you have that you believe God might use in some type of missions setting?

_____

_____

_____

"Whatever your hand finds to do, do it with all your might."
    –Ecclesiastes 9:10a

"Whatever you do, work at it with all your heart, as working for the Lord, not for men, since you know that you will receive an inheritance from the Lord as a reward. It is the Lord Christ you are serving."
    –Colossians 3:23-24

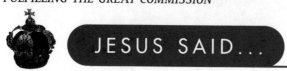

JESUS SAID...

Week 6, Day 3

TAKING A MAJOR STEP *continued . . .*

Opportunities in the area of career missions are vastly different than they once were. Traditionally, individuals or couples committing to career missions went overseas as young people, perhaps just out of college or seminary, and committed to spend their entire lives on the field. It was once believed that only younger people could learn foreign languages necessary to function overseas and that only young people could adapt cross-culturally.

This is no longer the case, however. Today many people are appointed as career missionaries when they are in their 40s and still have 15, 20, or 25 years left to serve overseas, in almost second vocations for them. They report great success in language learning and adjustment to life in new cultures. Missions agencies such as the International Mission Board have an "associate" category similar to a career missionary but which allows a person even in his or her 60s to participate.

Telling Buddhists about Christ is the post-retirement goal of Gary and Evelyn Harthcock. Both in their 80s, they use the Bible to teach English in a Southeast Asian country. Retired educators from North Carolina, the Harthcocks signed up for a short-term missions program. Some of their star pupils are Buddhist monks who come to them to learn English and in the process are taught that God made all things, including each one of them.

No longer is missions only for seminary-trained pastors and church-staff members. Lay persons have become tremendously successful overseas personnel. One such individual is Calvin Fox, a well-known Southern Baptist agriculturist in India, who has helped save a portion of India's population from starvation because of farming techniques he has taught them. As nationals flock to a center at which Fox and others teach agricultural skills, they also can learn about Jesus from Indian believers who teach there. At the International Mission Board, missionaries today draw on skills from more than 100 occupations. Many more are doing jobs for which they had no special training before God's call on their lives.

Once again, your financial freedom enables you to have more than just a passing interest in these choices. People who counsel with individuals and couples desiring missionary appointments report the heartbreak that results

Week 6, Day 3

when people feel God calling them to go, yet financial obligations prevent their going.

If reading these descriptions has done more than just pique your curiosity, I urge you to contact a missions agency for more information.[1] Your local church or the state or national offices of your denomination can tell you whom to write or call.

Take seriously any ways in which the Holy Spirit has spoken to you as you have read about this subject. Stop and pray, and ask God to make it clear to you how He wants you to bless the nations with the time, energy, and money He has made available to you.

[1] *For Missions Opportunities Through:*
    International Mission Board, call 1-800-866-3621
    North American Mission Board, call 1-770-410-6480

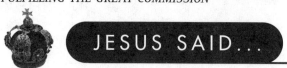

IGNITE THE FIRE AT HOME

Did I expand your horizons with some of the proposals in yesterday's study? Here's a new way to be a critical force in Great Commission work without leaving the shores of America.

You can be a **missions advocate**: the person in your local church who is a catalyst for everything your church does in the name of missions. Perhaps right now isn't the time for you to personally leave home and be a missionary in some other part of the country or world. Maybe you sincerely don't feel called to go. Perhaps you're waiting to become "empty-nested," or some other family or health situation keeps you tied down for now.

But this you do know: God has put a burning passion in your heart for the lost of the world. You're aware that He has blessed you for the purpose of your being His vessel for the Good News. As a missions advocate, your job is to make that passion contagious. After all, it only takes a spark to get a fire going, and you can become that spark!

As a missions advocate, you can literally turn your church into a Great Commission resource center — almost like a satellite office for a missions agency. You can be the person who serves on or chairs your church's missions committee or who acts as a missions liaison with the regional or state offices of your denomination.

Here are some things you can do in this capacity:

- Inspire your church to conduct missions fairs — exciting, colorful occasions in which the whole potpourri of missions opportunities available to your church is visible. People who have served overseas or who have been involved in some type of local missions work set up booths — sometimes offering sample foods from the region they represent, sometimes showing slides from work performed in God's name. The fair becomes an excellent recruitment vehicle for the next trip or project.

Week 6, Day 4

- Make certain the prayer ministry of your church keeps current missionary needs before it.

- Stock a display table in a high-traffic area of your church with leaflets and magazines about missions projects. Set up a world map on a focal wall; bullet places in the United States and on the globe where people from your church are serving/will serve/could serve.

- Alert members of your church about how to pray for missionaries in segments of the nation or world where earthquakes, floods, famine, bombings or other violence occurs, or where crucial political elections are being held.

- Make proposals at your church business meetings about adopting ethnic groups for prayer, communication, and other support, or adopting a segment of a city for missions work. An exciting approach these days is for some of the world's mega-cities, like Mexico City or Istanbul, to be divided into quadrants, with U. S. churches adopting a quadrant to focus on through prayer or missions trips. This makes the load lighter for on-site missionaries who need help in reaching the millions of lost people in such populous areas. You also could undertake this approach with your own city and adopt the quadrant in which your church is situated or another area.

- Serve on the board of trustees of your denomination's missions agency or on independent mission boards for specific needs.

- Serve as the church's missions "conscience," making certain that money is set aside through the annual budgeting process for missions trips or other projects.

- Help your church establish and furnish a missionary residence: a home in your community where missionaries can live, free of charge, during the period (often a year, although sometimes less) they are on stateside assignment.

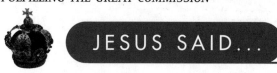

JESUS SAID...

Week 6, Day 4

IGNITE THE FIRE AT HOME *continued . . .*

- Be an advocate for people in your church who want to go overseas but haven't achieved the financial means to do so. You can match those who have needs with those (perhaps even yourself) who have an abundance to give.

- Be a watchdog on the church budget, making sure that funds appropriated for missions are actually being spent on missions causes.

- Help youth to plan fund-raisers, like yard sales and car washes, to enable them to take missions trips. You can use your free-enterprise skills to develop fund-raising techniques and multiply the way church finances are used for missions.

You are able to do this, of course, because of the sound financial practices you have acquired from your *Jesus On Money* study. The same healthy habits you use in managing your home budget can benefit your church and can ensure the Lord's money is used to its maximum capacity.

Have you ever done anything like this? Put a star by ways mentioned above that you have been/currently are involved. Perhaps you have thought of missions advocate tasks that I didn't mention. If so, list them here.

_____
_____
_____
_____

If none of these fits you, then be an encourager: someone who is willing to pray with people considering missions service, to write notes to people on the field (email is becoming a good way to communicate with missionaries anywhere), to provide child care for couples so they can attend missions information conferences. The ways to encourage are endless.

Ask God how He wants you to be personally involved in advocating missions in your church.

Week 6, Day 4

Write a brief prayer and ask God to lead you as you consider your role in spreading the good news, the gospel.

_____

_____

_____

_____

Notes

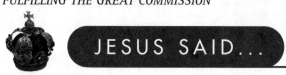

JESUS SAID...

Week 6, Day 5

This Week

SEND THE LIGHT

Numerous accounts indicate that in various corners of the world people are coming to faith in Christ in unprecedented numbers.

For example, do you know the story of Cambodia? That country became very much a victim of the Vietnam War. It was a traditionally Buddhist country, inheriting a government in the late 1970s that literally slaughtered millions of its own people. The "killing fields" became a trademark of Cambodia. However, as terrible as that was, God moved into Cambodia in surprising and incredible ways out of the ashes of that disaster. In the late 1980s, a few evangelical Christians began planting seeds here and there in Cambodia. These seeds grew, and a handful of new congregations sprang up rapidly, creating a base on which the Cambodian Baptist Convention was founded. Suddenly a spiritual explosion ignited, and churches started multiplying so rapidly that even the Cambodian Christians themselves couldn't keep count!

The same phenomenon has occurred in other places such as Mongolia, several of the former Soviet republics, and in a number of Muslim countries. Church planting movements are spreading rapidly around the world.

The communist government in China found that its policy of trying to stamp out Christianity boomeranged dramatically. When the persecution of Christians began in the early 1950s, Christians numbered less than one million. By the dawn of the 21st century, the number of Christians had swelled to some 70 to 80 million — more than seven percent of the entire Chinese population — and is continuing to grow rapidly.

The gospel is spreading even into countries where missionary activity is strictly forbidden, thanks to strategic work in "gateway" cities like London. Immigrants from other lands settle there to seek political asylum, a better life, or business opportunities. As the world comes to London, Christian workers attempt to plant churches among various people-group populations — like Turkish Kurds, Sikhs, Indian Hindus, and Muslims. When those internationals return home to visit relatives or to make business contacts, they often go as new believers who then can take the good news back — going places where Western missionaries would never be allowed.

Week 6, Day 5

Scripture Verses

Do you know any stories like this? Perhaps you've heard a missionary speak about great victories or dark portions of the world that are opening to the light of Christ. Perhaps you've read something awe-inspiring in a missions magazine or heard a praise report in a prayer meeting. Describe ways below that God is using Christians to push back the darkness.

_____

_____

_____

_____

Despite these advances, the sun will set tonight on people around the world who would have come to faith in Jesus if someone had simply been there to teach them in their own language! A letter circulating on the Internet purports to be from a lost person who has died in another country, gone to hell, and is writing back to ask Christians, "Why didn't you come and tell me?" The point of the letter is a dramatic reality check for any Christian. See what God desires of you in 2 Peter 3:9b.

" . . . He is patient with you, not wanting anyone to perish, but everyone to come to repentance."
–2 Peter 3:9b

God expects great obedience from the American church. No doubt wonderful accomplishments in obeying the Great Commission have occurred in churches across our land, and we have many victories to celebrate.

What do you count in your own life and in the life of your church and denomination as great victories? *(Example: I invited an international student to a worship service at my church. My church reported record baptisms last year.)*

_____

_____

_____

In the above exercise, I hope you were able to tally in a lifetime of tithing and giving to missions offerings on the national and international level. But you may have come to faith only in recent years. God has a wonderful plan for you and many victories yet to celebrate!

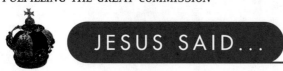

JESUS SAID...

SEND THE LIGHT *continued . . .*

Scripture Verses

"Therefore go and make disciples of all nations, baptizing them in the name of the Father and of the Son and of the Holy Spirit, and teaching them to obey everything I have commanded you. And surely I am with you always, to the very end of the age."
    –Matthew 28:19-20

"For God so loved the world that he gave his one and only Son, that whoever believes in him shall not perish but have eternal life."
    –John 3:16

I hope you also counted the number of people you have personally introduced to Christ as Savior. Do you know that number? _____

The question now is, how much more can you accomplish in the days that remain? With the average life expectancy lengthening, even if you are an older adult, those remaining days may be many. A whole wave of baby boomers are on the eve of retirement. In keeping with the trends of their previous years, boomers enter retirement desiring to find true meaning in life and to leave lasting legacies.

If we could challenge God's people to control their lifestyles and free up some resources — not to dissipate their savings but to take maybe one-fourth of their reserves — we could probably free up about $1 trillion. If we used those funds for missions, think what it would do for missions worldwide! Think how many people that sum would send, how many Bibles could be distributed, how many churches it would build in remote areas, and how many water wells it would dig so people could learn of the Living Water! God wants to use us as stewards to funnel His money from us into His kingdom, for the advancement of His good news.

The bottom line is this: financial freedom for the saints of God is directly linked to the salvation of souls. Think of it. Your individual budget is as important to funding kingdom enterprise as is the church budget — if not more so!

I can think of no greater motive for you to passionately pursue faithful stewardship in all matters than what the Bible succinctly teaches: God so loves the world that He has given His Son so that all will be saved for eternity.

May God bless you with wisdom and insight on your journey of faithful stewardship in this life. I pray He will speak these words over you when you stand before Him in glory — "Well done, good and faithful servant! . . . Come and share your master's happiness!" (Matthew 25:21).

Week 6, Day 5

Notes

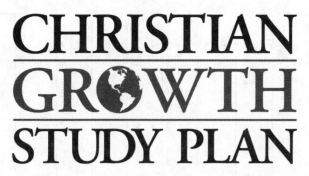

CHRISTIAN GROWTH STUDY PLAN

Preparing Christians to Serve

In the **Christian Growth Study Plan (formerly Church Study Course)**, this book *JESUS ON MONEY: CROSSING THE FINISH LINE* is a resource for course credit in the subject area **STEWARDSHIP** of the Christian Growth category of diploma plans. To receive credit, read the book, complete the learning activities, show your work to your pastor, a staff member or church leader, then complete the information on the next page. The form may be duplicated. Send the completed page to:

Christian Growth Study Plan

127 Ninth Avenue, North, MSN 117

Nashville, TN 37234-0117

FAX: (615)251-5067

For information about the Christian Growth Study Plan, refer to the current Christian Growth Study Plan Catalog. Your church office may have a copy. If not, request a free copy from the Christian Growth Study Plan office (615/251-2525).

JESUS ON MONEY: CROSSING THE FINISH LINE
COURSE NUMBER: CG - 0560

PARTICIPANT INFORMATION

Social Security Number (USA ONLY) | — | —

Personal CGSP Number*

Name (First, Middle, Last)

Date of Birth (MONTH, DAY, YEAR) | — | —

Home Phone | —

Address (Street, Route, or P.O. Box)

City, State, or Province

Zip/Postal Code

CHURCH INFORMATION

Church Name

Address (Street, Route, or P.O. Box)

City, State, or Province

Zip/Postal Code

CHANGE REQUEST ONLY

☐ Former Name

☐ Former Address

City, State, or Province

Zip/Postal Code

☐ Former Church

City, State, or Province

Zip/Postal Code

Signature of Pastor, Conference Leader, or Other Church Leader

Date

*New participants are requested but not required to give SS# and date of birth. Existing participants, please give CGSP# when using SS# for the first time. Thereafter, only one ID# is required. **Mail to:** Christian Growth Study Plan, 127 Ninth Ave., North, Nashville, TN 37234-0117. Fax: (615)251-5067

Rev. 6-99

128